Lifted at the GATE

"A Story of Hopelessness to Hope"

By:

AYODEJI **MEGBOPE**

First Printing: October 2019

Proudly Nigerian

digitalreality
PRINT LIMITED
...awesome images

0812 992 3786 , 0708 860 2610, +234 708 860 2608
www.digitalrealityprintlimited.com

Table of Contents

Dedication

─────⊙o⊙o─────

I dedicate this book to everyone out there who has been labelled, called a non-achiever, had a rough past, struggling in one area or the other. I dedicate this book to everyone that has defied all odds and have gone ahead to break barriers. I dedicate this book to everyone who is holding on and waiting for their breakthrough season.

Do not be weary, keep pressing, keep working, keep praying, that breakthrough will come if you refuse to quit.

I thank God Almighty for the gift of His son Jesus Christ. Thank you Olufemi Adedayo Megbope, my darling husband of 26 years. Thank you Olukorede and Abisola Megbope our precious children, you have not allowed us to cover our heads in shame.

To my siblings, my husband's siblings, my dad, mother-in-law and to the blessed memories of my beloved mother and father-in-law, I say thank you. My precious daughter, Igwehi Fidelia Esharefasa, you painstakingly edited this book despite your very busy schedule, I love and deeply appreciate you. Tosin Ade Ajayi, you kept pushing, thank you for your patience. Imisioluwa Owolabi, lover of God's presence, thank you for your priceless contribution.

My life has been impacted by a lot of you in ways too numerous to mention. A special thank you to Bishops Mike and Peace Okonkwo, Pastors Taiwo and Nomthi Odukoya, all my friends and mentors. Thank you Mrs Folorunso Alakija for making this book a reality.

Foreword

Life is never a straight journey; it is full of curves and twists, hills and valleys, ups and downs. Often, those who make a success of this journey are those who through determination and courage have learnt to build castles with the bricks life throws at them. The truth is, stories abound of women who have risen from the depths of despair and discouragement to become beacons of success in various areas of endeavour. This book contains one of such story. It is the story of a woman who, in spite of the numerous challenges on her path, refused to give up.

Though her story has been told in many places and even used as a case study in some schools, I do not think the nitty-gritty of how she became the success she is today has ever been told the way she has done in this book. The book tells of her rise from the depth of the valley and desperation to the mountaintop. Her courage in the face of fear and seeming defeat, her strength in the face of overwhelming weakness, and her hope in the place where everything was beckoning to her to give up will encourage and inspire you.

I have known Ayodeji Megbope for many years and was privy, especially as her pastor, to some of the challenges she faced in her journey to greatness. Her determination, unalloyed commitment to God and family, and her refusal to surrender to despair stand out among her many qualities. Her story is brilliantly told in this book, and it is exciting and easy to read. Above all, it offers valuable lessons for everyone who desires to make a success of his or her business and life generally.

I wholeheartedly recommend it.

Taiwo Odukoya
Senior Pastor
The Fountain of Life Church
Ilupeju, Lagos Nigeria

/////////////////////////////////
Chapter One
/////////////////////////////////

Born Like Any Other

I was born into a Christian home and the second of five children. My father, Ekundayo Olumuyiwa Ogunmekan worked as an Engineer and my mum of blessed memory was a full-time home maker. Dad later in life became a clergy man in the Anglican Communion and rose to the enviable rank of an Archdeacon. I was born in Ilorin, Kwara State, on the 6th of September 1968, a date very close to the birth of my elder sister who was born on the 1st of September 1967. I have fond memories of my siblings and I growing up in Kano as dad was transferred there being an employee with the Federal Government. It was fun growing up in Kano, because it was a state known for trading and large-scale farming, which meant that food was not only cheap, but equally available and in surplus. Dad was a disciplinarian to the core, a no-nonsense but loving man. He would discipline us yet love us.

Dad laid tremendous emphasis on godliness and sound education. He bent over backwards to ensure he gave all five of us equal opportunities in life. My dear mother of blessed memory was also quite tough but equally loving. I particularly got whipped a lot because I was quite a puzzle to handle.

As a full-time home maker, my mother, Mrs. Abiodun Olufunmilayo Ogunmekan spared nothing at ensuring her family was well nourished and protected. She indeed wanted the best for us. I laugh as I recall some memories of her zealousness all in attempting to give us the best. Ours was a very close-knit family; no child was treated differently from the other. Our parents loved each other dearly, they were great friends and kept nothing from each other. This made it very difficult to get away with mischief. They were both in the know on everything and always on the same page about everything. I grew up wishing one of them would have a difference in opinion but that was never to be. I watched my mother live her life in total submission to my father. Whatever he said was law. I always thought she was indeed blessed to be married to a good man. If married to a tyrant, any woman having her kind of overtly submissive attitude would never live a fulfilling life, I used to think to myself. Not only was my mother submissive, she was totally content with anything she had, and she ensured she passed this virtue to every one of her children. My father's heart indeed safely trusted in her.

Their love for each other was palpable and this ensured a lot of peace and stability in the family. Even when things were tough, my mother stood by my father like a rock. She was always there for him and indeed for all her children. Her limited exposure sometimes ended us in a fix. A typical example was when a neighbor of ours returned from a trip abroad. It was our neighbor's normal practice to return from her trip with little items for every member of our family. She bought two lovely flowery "gowns", one for my sister and one for me. We were both eleven and ten years respectively and we couldn't wait to wear them. Mum told us they were church outfits and because they were terribly transparent she needed to get us nice inner garments. The "gowns" had a white background with lovely little flowers all over them. My darling mum made pink inner garments because the gowns had pink trimmings round the neck. The D-day to "launch" our beautiful "gowns" came. We had shiny black shoes and white socks that we thought provided a perfect match for the gown and black hats to give us that fitting "church child" look. Off to church we went, feeling like we were making a fashion statement.

On returning home that day, we handed over our beautiful gowns to mum for safe keep and could not contain our excitement when mum told us that she would be going to see her friend later that evening. We pleaded with her to take us along so we could thank her friend for the lovely dresses. Our horror was unimaginable when on arriving mum's friend's house, we saw her daughter in the same "gown" we had worn to church. On asking if they were going out, her mum replied that she was getting ready for bed. "Can't you see she's in her nightgown?", mum's friend asked.

My mum, my sister and I looked at one another and went quiet. "No wonder the fabric is so thin and transparent," I whispered to my sister who couldn't stop shaking her head. They say, "what you don't know will not kill you", but I always respond, "Not so fast; what you do not know might just embarrass you". No wonder The Bible admonishes in Ecclesiastes 7:25. "I applied mine heart to know, and to search, and to seek out wisdom, and the reason of things". Such was my mum's devotion to her children, always wanting us to come out looking the best, every way she knew how.

Mum was always there for us all. She was undoubtedly stern and very spiritual. In those days, I thought that she hated me because of the spanking, scolding and monitoring I received from her, all in a bid to ensure I turned out right. Years had passed before I began to truly appreciate her for trying to train me to be responsible. The impact she made in my life was truly remarkable. After my mum passed on, several childhood experiences began to flood my mind. I recall when I was fourteen, mum found a love letter from my boyfriend. I knew there was no telling what my mother could do. I had braced myself for the worst beating of my life. My mother could be trusted to always be creative with her mode of discipline. This time around, she responded by walking me to the barbers to have my hair shaved off, insisting that the barber further adorn my scalp with oil and then ordering me to follow her as she marched me round some streets in our neighborhood, including of course the street where the boy lived.

I cried bitterly at the stares and mocking jeers I received from amused neighbors. Holding my mother's photograph and remembering how strict she was with me all those years, all I can say is, "Thank you Jesus for the hands that helped to shape my life". I learnt early in life that when we groan under the pain and discomfort of discipline, reproof or correction, we ought to consider them as 'light afflictions' which lasts only for a moment, working for us a far more exceeding and eternal weight of glory, and choosing not to look at the things which we see but at the things which we do not see - for the things which we see are temporal, but the things which we do not see are eternal. (2 Corinthians 4:17). Indeed, glory awaits us as we go through the shadows of pain.

//////////////////////////////////
Chapter Two
//////////////////////////////////

Oppressed and Depressed

My parents were truly wonderful. They taught us godly living and the need to value education above everything else. In those days, I was so naïve about a lot of things, maybe because of the many challenges I experienced while growing up. I doubted myself a lot and was bullied in school. There were times I knew in my heart what to do, but because of the abuse, bullying and intimidation I experienced, I walked away from doing them. For example, I knew I was skilled at debates; I had guts and intelligence. I also knew I could volunteer to read in class, but the bullying and abuse was so intense that I lost my self-worth. I thought that no one loved or cared for me. The pain it brought to me was very deep.

My experience in the hands of bullies, oppressors and abusers taught me life lessons and prepared me a great deal for parenting. I realized that parents must ensure they are not just physically present with their children. There is a need to constantly engage them, allow them to express themselves, be mindful about who we leave them with and never take anything for granted. There is a constant need to probe and try to find out what's happening in their lives. Children need to be constantly followed up so that as parents, we can be up-to-date with happenings in their lives.

To know what is going on in our children's lives, we as parents need to develop intimacy with them and this requires a great deal of communication. We must talk to them, listen to them, and ask relevant questions especially when strange patterns begin to show up in their lives. It is never enough to give them a list of dos and don'ts. We need to talk to them and listen to them - with our ears, eyes and our hearts. When a child is going through a crisis, there are always red flags. Unfortunately, some parents are too busy to notice them or completely clueless on how to handle them. We need to ask them questions and give them a sense of assurance and security and let them know that we really care about them. We ought to always be there for them even when they do wrong things, and to show them love even as we discipline them.

I have realized that the rod is not always the solution to correcting a child's misdemeanor. It is important to let our children be aware that we are always there for them in the good and the bad times. As parents, our duty requires that we protect and love them unconditionally. We should avoid implanting fear into them as it will only cause the child to withdraw. Parents must pay the price to spend quality time with their children.

Long before our children arrived, my husband and I had agreed that we were going to pay the price of raising our children ourselves. My bitter experience of abuse even in a secure environment made us more resolute about this. We had to make sacrifices especially as we became aware that there is no parenting without pain. Sometimes, people we bring into our homes become a problem. Instead of helping, they bring more chaos into our lives. I struggled very hard with my academics. I had several distractions which affected my performance. I had a lot in me to contend with. A lot of negative occurrences happened around me that affected my self-esteem horribly. I had very low self-esteem. I always found myself getting into trouble. Sometimes, the trouble came to me, at other times, I walked into it. I found myself passionately loving negative adventure.

I wasn't living a completely immoral life with my hard-fought freedom; I was just a rebel who wanted to be heard and loved. I wanted my fears allayed, I wanted my confidence restored and I wanted my pain smoothened. Unfortunately, I expressed all these desires in ways that annoyed, exasperated and confused my mother. I obviously went about my one-man protest the wrong way. I thought I would be heard and understood by being daring and adventurous, but it didn't happen. I ended up getting into more trouble. In my teenage years, I had boyfriends just like other young girls. I was really trying to understand the meaning of life. I did not drink or smoke; all I craved for was to be accepted. As a matter of fact, I started keeping boyfriends because my friends were also having them. I did not have any sense of fulfillment. I did not believe in myself because I was helplessly insecure. I knew I could do quite a lot of things, but I simply did not do any excellently.

I was timid and shy and was always booed and intimidated by friends who noticed my lack of self-confidence. They would often ridicule and laugh at me. Those were experiences that made me fearful and depressed. I personally do not believe any human being deserves to be oppressed and harassed. We all need to be loved and cared for. Those were the things I craved, but I got the opposite. Fear totally engulfed my life, and almost killed the talents and endowments I had. I didn't want to continue to be harassed and oppressed, so I kept to myself a lot and never had the courage to allow my talents free expression because of the happenings around me. Being alone made me feel good because there was no one around to mock, taunt or talk me down. I would give myself pass marks for the dexterity in talking to myself and the mirror. Sometimes mum would catch me either dancing or debating in front of a mirror and just shake her head at the vanity of dancing without music or talking to myself. At times, she was upset at me, but what she did not know was that it was paradise for me, and a way to express myself freely.

I did not have serious dreams even though I was surrounded by siblings who had huge dreams and ambitions. My case appeared different as I was extremely playful. My playfulness was a coping mechanism to suppress my pain and this especially bothered my mum. Playing helped to conceal a lot of insecurities within me.

When I wrote my first West African Examination Council Examination, I obtained four credits. This was not good enough for my dad and he encouraged me to make a second attempt at it. My second attempt was dismal. I came out of it with a pass in English Language and failures in the other subjects. This terribly upset my parents. The blame was completely mine because I kept a lot of bad company, was a truant in school and did not attend lectures when I should have. The Bible says we reap what we sow. Since I wasn't serious with my academics, I truly reaped failure. We must however realize that failure does not exist until we give up.

Recalling this bit of my past reminds me of the developmental milestones our own children went through in the process of getting to walk. From crawling to standing, from standing to taking baby steps, from taking baby steps to finally and getting their feet firm on the ground, they were all over the place before we knew it. However, during all these metamorphoses, they stumbled at one point or the other. It was their getting up after stumbling that eventually helped them to stand on their two feet and take charge of their lives. There are stages we need to courageously go through in life if we are ever going to fulfil purpose and if we are ever going to discover the different gifts in us. Fall many times we may but get up every time we must. What matters most is the discovery and the continuing to discover. "For a just man falleth seven times, and riseth up again" (Proverbs 24:16a KJV).

It took many years for me to heal emotionally, mentally, spiritually and psychologically. My healing process started when I had to be brutally frank with myself that the past had happened, the evils had taken place, and there was no way I could re-write it. So, I had to let it all go. I had to let the pains of the past go. The word of God says we should forget the former things, which includes our pains and hurts and look forward to the new things He would do. God has indeed been faithful. The pain and the shame of the past have become tools of strength for me not only to improve my life but the lives of those around me. When I see some of my past crazy and reckless behaviors showing up in the life of a young person, I am more empathic towards their plight and I try as much as it lies within my power to counsel them out of it.

Everything that has happened to me has been a lesson. It has made me a better person; a better wife; a better mother; a better counselor; a better business woman; a better Christian. Having been through hurt myself, I can feel for those who are passing through similar issues. I have been able to counsel people of all ages on how to heal from their pain and heartache and most importantly, walk away from them. The solution lies in giving it all to Jesus, and leaving it with Him, for He truly and sincerely cares for us. When we give the Lord our pain and challenges, He gives us His peace, and courage to face life like a soldier who knows that the battle ahead has already been won. I always emphasize how critically important it is for parents to ensure that they listen to their children, believe in them, affirm them and most importantly be there for them even when the chips are down.

Chapter Three

A Crisis of Identity

My teenage years were full of identity crises. For most of my teenage years, I just existed and did not know who I really was or what my purpose on earth was. I just took every day as it came. When my second Secondary School Certificate Examination result came out again with poor grades, dad literarily sent me out of the house. He asked me to take a long walk and then return to tell him what I wanted to do with my life. After very deep thinking and assessment of my chances, and having stumbled on a typing and shorthand school, I went back to him and informed him that I wanted to learn how to type and write in shorthand. As soon as I started attending that school I was "crowned queen" of typing and shorthand. However, I was aware that I only excelled because I was in an environment that was way below my potentials. My high grades in the school did not impress my dad so much because he knew only too well that there was more to me than typing and shorthand.

Having spent some time in the first typing school, I moved on to a proper Secretarial College. It was a government-recognized institute known as Grace Institute (now Grace Polytechnic). It was there I obtained a Higher Diploma in Secretarial Administration. My dad saw the changes that had begun to occur in my life and academics and encouraged me to do more – to go a step higher and not be content with mediocrity. He encouraged me to take to the next level what I had begun to put together. I had moved from being indifferent and playful to becoming serious with my life and studies, and the result was there for everyone to see. I had sown hard work and commitment, and I was starting to reap success in my Secretarial course. In life, we must make every effort to move to the next level, for as long as there is life in us, there is always something more. I am grateful to God that my father's faith and confidence in me increased and from that point, I started experiencing a turnaround. My grades were constantly high, and I began to blossom. I was glad that I was finally getting positive results from doing something. I was receiving praise and affirmation and my confidence level had started growing. I did not care anymore who liked me or who did not. I focused more on being a better me. Gradually, I began to let go of the hurt and bitterness I used to feel. Nobody thrives in a hostile environment. Sometimes, a change of environment is just what we need to be delivered from the pain and rejection of the past. My fear of what people thought of me started to lose its grip on me. I realized that people would only get at me if I allowed them to. I learnt that everybody is entitled to their opinion and until I became preoccupied with building my life, their opinion of me would prevent me from moving forward.

I had been so surrounded by many naysayers in my life that I was hindered severally from stepping out to do things that I had always wanted to do. Back in school, I was constantly jeered and booed at whenever I tried to do anything; the fear of it had crippled me and prevented me for a long time. However, I recall that on a particular occasion, I had decided to come out of my shadows and volunteer to represent my class for a debate despite fears of what might come during or after the debate. I took part in the debate, and just outside the class were two known bullies waiting for me. Scared to my wits, they led me outside. One of them turned to me, pulled my ear and whispered, "You did great at the debate." I was terribly scared and stood there not even able to look them in the eye. After a few minutes, without knowing where the strength came from, I looked up, smiled and said "thank you". I walked away from them with a smile, I gave myself a pat on the back for mustering the courage to finally step out of the shadows. Learning to rid myself of toxic people became a priority to me. This was hard for me, but I knew I just had to walk away from some relationships.

Life in the shadows is a miserable place to be. There is so much liberty in living life out of the shadows. The moment I decided to walk away from people who considered me not good enough for them was the moment I started appreciating myself and the little abilities inside of me and it was then that my life began to take a dramatic turn. My eyes began to open to the fact that I indeed had something to offer. Everybody has something to offer! Time wasted in hiding in the shadows of our past, our weaknesses, our lack or our critics cannot be recycled. Little wonder The Bible says to us to "walk circumspectly, not as fools, but as wise, redeeming the time" (Ephesians 5:15 KJV). Gifts and talents come from God. It is in our making use of these gifts that they multiply. Likewise, it is in the lack of use of our gifts and talents that we begin to lose them. Most importantly, the more we desire the Giver of the gifts, the more of His attention we get. God has no favorites. The number and types of gifts He gives to every man is entirely His prerogative. Worthy of emphasis, however is the fact that the mastery or increase of our gifts, talents or abilities is determined by whether (and by how much) we use them. Even much more than natural gifts is the priceless Gift of the Presence of God. His Presence in us increases only as we place a demand on Him. It increases as we pay the price of withdrawing from the crowd to seek His face. Then, God's voice becomes more audible and recognizable to us. We can then hear Him say to us, "This is the way, walk ye in it." (Isaiah 30:21).

////////////////////////////////

Chapter Four

////////////////////////////////

Can I Really Forgive?

The courage to walk away from the bondage of pleasing others and the liberty to no longer crave to be liked by everyone was like a breath of fresh air. It was indeed liberating and energizing. However, my speed was hindered. It was not difficult to find what caused that to happen. Unforgiveness was the culprit! I would take a few steps with confidence and end up limping whenever I recalled some incidents from the past. I began to pray to God to help me forgive my abusers and my healing became rapid! I soon realized that the confirmation of my healing would be tested by a confrontation. I discovered that as much as I did not have to relate anymore with some people who had taken advantage of me in the past, there were a few I kept bumping into.

I succeeded in ignoring some of them however, there were one or two I kept encountering. My encounter with them would always leave me feeling vulnerable, depressed, bitter and vengeful. Worse still was the fact that they were family. I would deploy tactics like avoiding family functions, leaving family functions abruptly and keeping a low profile to avoid these meetings. All of these left me feeling caged and I wondered when I would eventually be at liberty to attend family functions without feeling like a victim. I knew I felt this way because I was still living in unforgiveness, even though I had gotten my self-esteem back and my life was beginning to take shape. I felt I deserved an apology from the person who stole my innocence but then, I began to ask myself if I was going to stay bitter for an apology that might never come. I learnt that forgetting and forgiving were two totally different things. I discovered that I needed to forgive so that I could be totally delivered from the sting of my past.

Praying for grace to forgive became the only option for me and as I prayed, I began to actually feel sorry for those people I had labelled "my abusers."

Remember what I said earlier about realizing that the confirmation of my healing would be tested by a confrontation? The D-day came at a social function. It was initially an awkward moment for me, but I quickly reminded myself that I was no longer a slave to the bondage of unforgiveness. I hadn't seen my abuser in years. The truth was that I had deliberately avoided him but that day was different. I had become another woman, I had taken my deliverance to another level by being able to bring myself to a point where I no longer felt spiteful and vengeful. Rather I began to feel pity and sympathy for this person whose mind was depraved. I concluded that he was the one in the bondage and chain of sin and insanity and he needed to be helped. Having my husband and my children (who all knew the episode) with me was so strengthening.

It felt liberating as I found myself walking confidently towards him and giving him a broad smile. This obviously disarmed him. As I introduced my husband and children to him, I could see that he felt very uncomfortable. My husband gave him a firm handshake and we all walked away. It was an unforgettable moment of priceless triumph and joy. I left that function that day feeling like I had won a lottery. Free at last! I exhaled to myself! I'm no longer a slave to my past! A year or so later when I bumped into this fellow again, I was called to give a short speech at a function we both attended. The ovation accorded me when I was done was almost deafening. This time around, he couldn't contain himself. He walked up to me as I made my way to my seat. "Ayo! You've done so well for yourself, please forgive me, I'm deeply sorry for the past". I smiled, "the past is gone, I've put all that behind me", I responded. Amazing! The apology I had waited for all these years came only as I forgave first!

Were you abused? Are you still fighting to overcome the hurt of abuse? It is time to let go, dear friend! You cannot undo yesterday. Nobody has the ability to do that. Rehearsing the past will only allow the abuser to meet you where he left you! Letting go of the past is the sign of our preparedness for a better tomorrow. Instead of allowing the past label me a victim of child abuse, I have chosen to be a voice against this evil. Forgiving is a necessity for our breakthrough and we have consolation in the bible as it tells us in Isaiah 43:18-19 (KJV), "Remember ye not the former things, neither consider the things of old. Behold, I will do a new thing; now it shall spring forth; shall ye not know it? I will even make a way in the wilderness and rivers in the desert."

///////////////////////////////

Chapter Five

///////////////////////////////

Empowered to Live and Love

I want to take a step back to talk about one encounter that was revolutionary for me. That encounter was meeting with and accepting Jesus Christ into my life. It brought me unprecedented change; my life took on a new dimension. I was born into a Christian family, but I found out that being born into one was not a guarantee of a personal relationship with Christ. Initially, I didn't see any need to take this step as I considered myself to be a Christian already. Growing up with my parents ensured that the discipline of timeliness and total commitment to anything we were involved in was instilled in us. This of course included church activities like Sunday service, society meetings in church, going through 'confirmation classes' as an Anglican, taking Holy Communion and the likes. I saw myself as a church girl and found no need to make any new confession. However, I recall attending an evening church service with a friend of mine and hearing the pastor preach about "A new life in Christ Jesus." As he carefully preached on the death, burial and resurrection of Jesus Christ, I knew that I had been living my life not really knowing the sacrifice that had been made for me on Calvary. I realized the need to deliberately step out to make a confession of receiving Jesus Christ and acknowledging Him as my personal Lord and Savior. I felt peace, joy and hope and from then on, the avalanche of the word of God I continued to receive from the ministry of Bishop Mike Okonkwo began to impact my life profoundly. After graduating from school, I began work in 1989. My first job was as a Senior Confidential Secretary to the Financial Manager of the then Federated Motor Industries. The job was a very interesting one and my first boss impacted my life significantly. While on the job, he became a father figure but this did not come without some initial drama.

When I first began working with him, I was apprehensive. My experience was an emotional roller-coaster ride, half-expecting that I would be rejected again, but thoroughly enjoying work. However, my confidence had begun to grow because of the word of God I had started to feed on, and this quickly dispelled any negative feelings of fear. My boss was a no nonsense, strict perfectionist. His impression of me after my first few weeks of working with him was that I was a clumsy, naive, bloody secretary. As far as he was concerned, I had stretched his endurance capacity to the limit. True! He was a Senior Manager in the organization and he didn't deserve a greenhorn like me. His nasty remarks always made me cry and this further infuriated him. He added the adjective of "cry baby" to the names he called me. Little did I know that all the bosses I worked with were serving as tutors and governors, until the appointed time when the right character to sustain my blessing would have been deeply ingrained in me. I have gone through several endurance tests and I now know that these tests are what have become catalysts to my meeting, wining and dining with kings.

It indeed is no fable when The Bible talks about kings being our nursing fathers and queens being our nursing mothers. My first job laid a solid foundation for a twenty-year work experience that was ahead of me. Little did I know that these twenty years of working in three different major organizations were going to be filled with incidents, friends, foes, pains and victories - tools that I would need for a glorious future. One of the things that life has taught me is that things do not just happen. People do not just come into your life for nothing. There is a purpose for every relationship. However, it becomes our responsibility to recognize that purpose. Realizing the power that I had in Christ, I began to pray that God would change my story. I prayed that God would bring people into my life who would build me up. I knew that part of the problem I had gone through in life had been from associating with the wrong people. I had been held back by people who were visionless and going nowhere and who wanted others to go nowhere. It just made sense to me that if I wanted a change, then I needed to start associating with the right people. I earnestly asked the Lord to bring new people into my life who would challenge me and motivate me to be a better person. I desired a life with meaning; I wanted a life of significance.

Marriage became the next most important step that I needed to take. At a point, I was in a relationship that I was very unsure of. He was a nice guy, lover of God and he cared for me. He was serious minded but in spite of all that, I just was not satisfied. I could touch one or two aspects of our relationship I was not comfortable with and I felt we could work round it but the harder I tried to ignore these areas the more it became a big deal to me. Seeking the counsel of two of my closest friends did not help matters either. They felt I was looking for a 'Mr. Perfect' and made statements like "He's a nice guy" and "You will adjust." Statements like that left me more confused. I found myself happy today and unhappy the next day. I found myself having mood swings; I found myself comparing my relationship with others and I felt completely stuck especially with the Christianized statement, "He loves the Lord".

As time went on, I discovered that the fact that a guy is a Christian does not automatically mean that he is the right marriage partner for any Christian lady. I realized that some of the signs to confirm to you that you are in a relationship with the right guy for marriage are, you are convinced you can work things out, you are completely comfortable in your own skin when with him, you are not irritated, you are proud of him, you can see the future with him, you can talk about anything, you feel at peace, you don't have to pretend, you highly respect him and much more. I could only put a pass mark on about thirty percent of these and I knew without a doubt that we were both wasting each other's time and emotions. I wanted out, but it was tough especially as it appeared I was the only one who felt the way I did. It had begun to appear like I was sinking into the pit I had come out of before and I needed to snap out of it. I had overcome the bondage of wanting to please others and not wanting to hurt others at the expense of my joy and I had had enough. I needed strength to make this delicate move especially since he was really nice, had not hurt me and professed to love me deeply. I knew I was on my own as far as consulting anybody was concerned. The only option I knew I could trust was to pray about it. I knew I could trust God with all my issues. I knew no part of my life was out of bounds to Him. I knew He was more interested in my joy than anyone was. True to what I believed, God did make a way. He made breaking up easy and I became free at last.

Sometimes, we are actually very close to our miracles without realizing it. We pray to God over our needs, tell Him our desires, cry to Him when it appears to be taking forever and we become insensitive when He presents us with an answer. As soon as I became aware of this I became more deliberate in listening to God and knowing when He speaks to me. Little wonder my prayer to God for a husband of His will was answered in such a simple way. I am really grateful to God that I was not insensitive to His will for my life in this area.

It was an afternoon like any other, but I did not realize that a major encounter was going to take place. My regular visits to my friend's house that day turned out to be a special one as I exchanged pleasantries with her brother outside their house before eventually seeing her. Our casual conversation on that day evolved into marriage about two years after. Fast-forward twenty-six years, here we are, blessed with two adult children whose lives are daily glorifying God. When I look back and take stock of my life, I remain eternally grateful to God that I married my friend.

Before our wedding, we had a plan of the type of home we wanted to build. We had a picture of what we desired even though we did not quite know how everything would fit in. We spent courtship praying, playing, discussing, planning, preparing and learning from great examples. We had similar values, so it was easy for us to agree on a lot of things. God helped us (and still helps us) to stick to our plans. Sticking to our original plan has come amid severe setbacks, pain, tears, frustrations and discouragements. However, we keep holding hands believing God to see us through.

Getting married was not amidst pomp and pageantry. Regardless of the lack of grandeur however, we were very happy. We reminded ourselves that what makes a beautiful marriage is not a flamboyant wedding ceremony but two beautiful faith-filled hearts coming together. At our wedding reception, we could not afford to serve our guests with the usual wide variety of meals you get at wedding parties as we were bent on giving only what we could afford to give. We informed our families and friends about our wedding by word of mouth instead of printing wedding cards because there were other pressing needs. The program for the service was typed and photocopies made at a business center because that was what we would afford. We invested the little resources at our disposal and monetary gifts that came from family and friends on getting a decent accommodation and furnishing it. That was priority to us. We made choices because we knew that purposeful living was not about impressing others but about getting our priorities right.

One would think that getting it right from day one was a guarantee that troubles would not come along the way. For us as a family, life has not exactly been a bed of roses; it has been full of ups and downs but amidst it all, God has been undeniably faithful. I unashamedly admit that a while after we got married, we had to start selling our wedding gifts to keep the family going and to settle our bills. We couldn't tell anyone, not even our siblings; it was just between my husband and me. I recall about two years after our wedding, I sat in my room with tears in my eyes, bringing out what appeared to be the last set of our wedding presents. They were the best of the gifts we had received, and I had hoped they wouldn't go the way the others did. The pain was deep, but we kept believing that the sun would shine again.

At such times, there is that temptation to feel abandoned by friends and begin to live in bitterness. It was a roller coaster of battles and victories, but it dawned on us that everybody had a cross to carry and the earlier we took up our cross and fixed our eyes on Jesus, the better it would be for us. We knew that permanent help could only come from God, so it was easy for us to take our eyes off man. After all, nobody owed us anything.

I also recall about a year after our son was born, he fell ill, and we rushed him to the hospital. Just as he was being attended to by the doctor, we received a call from home that our apartment was on fire. The journey back home that day appeared to take forever. On getting home, we found out that our apartment had been forced into by neighbors who helped to put out the fire. The fire started in the kitchen from an electrical surge that affected the freezer. Our kitchen was severely affected but we knew there was great cause to thank God that the damage was not worse and there was no loss of life. I remember my husband holding me tightly as I sobbed, reminding me that God was in control. At that point, I was almost doubting God's love for us. I must have felt what Job felt when he said in Job 3:23 (KJV): "Why is light given to a man whose way is hid, and whom God hath hedged in?" Even though my husband was trying to be brave, we truly felt hedged in. Life was tough; we couldn't even pay our basic bills. This incident was one straw that was hard enough to break the camel's back.

////////////////////////////////

Chapter Six

////////////////////////////////

Thorns in My Roses

I went through these incidents feeling extremely vulnerable. My husband and I were at a point where we knew that except God kept us, we could not keep ourselves. We all have those moments when we know that if God does not come through, we would most likely want to take some compromising actions which we know would mess up our lives, our testimony and leave us at the mercy of mockers and jesters who had been waiting for us to trip, so that they can pounce on us and consume us like a pack of wolves. Such moments are really delicate because even though we know these truths, that desire we have can become so overwhelming that we might become completely flustered.

During those vulnerable seasons, my husband and I intentionally surrounded ourselves with God-fearing family, friends and people who we knew would genuinely uphold and encourage us and not laugh at us or take advantage of our vulnerability. My husband and I became very conscious of the need to deliberately shield ourselves from people we were not sure of.

It became very clear to us that the glorious future ahead of us – not our immediate need – was worth focusing on. This realization was what gave us strength to stand through this period. Indeed, we have had tough times in our marriage – times when we wished we could just hunker down somewhere till the storm was over; times of financial distress, despair, fear of tomorrow, anxiety over raising our children and many more. It was amid these several storms that we met different people who were also going through their own storms.

When life's storms bring people your way, you need to figure out what they are in your life for. Some come in as blessings from God and some come in as distractions to further distance you from your destination. People come into your life for a reason, a season or a lifetime. When you figure out which one it is, you will know how to determine boundaries. What helps you accurately discern who and who not to accommodate in your stormy season is whether or not they are adding any value to your life. They should help you to grow and learn. They should bring you an unbelievable amount of joy, succor, strength and peace. Such friends will prove to be massive tools in the hands of God to ensure we do not fall by the wayside but steadfastly continue in our life assignment. Never grant access to "energy vampires" - people you associate with who leave you feeling drained, or "flakey people" – people who excitedly make plans with you but are never committed enough to follow through. These two categories of people will not hesitate to throw you under the bus, so you do not need them. Remember, your friendships are really a reflection of who you are. Those you allow into your life in your stormy seasons become a critical part of you.

God helped us to get our priorities in marriage right and straight from day one. It was, and still is, God first and us second. We looked forward to the children coming and we knew their place in our priority list came next. Our eyes have always been focused - there were lots of things we did not have but we were absolutely full of the love we had for each other. Our trust in God made everything we didn't have insignificant. We knew we would get them all at the right time. I am very glad that twenty-six years after, the story has not changed. There were times however that delays began to get the better part of me. In our first seven years of marriage, we could not afford to buy a car. We were struggling financially and as much as the love was intact, the absence of basic needs began to weigh me down. I began to wonder if there was something wrong with us. My husband kept reminding me of God's faithfulness. I had heard sayings like "love without money is annoyance" and in my subconscious, I began to manifest this saying. I quickly got a hold of myself and refocused my attention on God and He did come through at the right time.

There is an aspect of a waiting season that I would like to focus on right here. Like I said earlier, God came through by supplying our needs, but I found out that one can get very complacent in a waiting season that you no longer have the strength or expectation for what you desire. When you have waited on God for something and you get to a point of unusual discomfort or anxiety, as a child of God, it is an indication that the answer is around the corner. There are therefore attitudes we need to adopt. The attitude of thanksgiving, the attitude of earnest expectation, the attitude of joy and the attitude of having our ears and eyes open to instructions and opportunities are must-haves. If we are not discerning in this critical season, we will begin to display attitudes that will delay our breakthrough, take the shine off the breakthrough when it comes, cause us to compromise and to seek for ungodly alternatives or sometimes make us completely lose the breakthrough. Having a right attitude in every situation puts us in a position of preparedness to receive. Remember, preparation is the eye that sees opportunities.

Never to be forgotten was the day we took a compulsory one-hour walk because we lacked One Hundred Naira to transport ourselves to my parents' house to pick our children who had stayed the weekend with them. We left home that day refusing to touch the tithe of almost a thousand naira we had put aside. Rather, we chose to "see" the faithfulness of our God. All through the walk, I had tears streaming down my face while my dear husband kept saying, "it is well." The sun was scorching, and just as I was wondering if we were really going to walk all the way to our destination, someone we knew drove by and gave us a lift. Our God came through!

I have taken time to share a few of several down times we had in our twenty-six-year-old marriage to encourage couples out there that marriage comes with the good and the not-too-good. It is however important to remember that as children of God, ALL things work together for our good. Hebrews 10:36 (KJV) says: "For ye have need of patience, that, after ye have done the will of God, ye might receive the promise." Hearing other people's experiences and testimonies helped us a great deal and I pray that the few I have shared and will be sharing in this book will encourage you. Diligently rejoicing at the testimonies of others always helps to increase our strength and boost our faith. If God did it for one, it is an indication of what He will do for as many as put their trust in Him. The Bible says: "Let us hold fast the profession of our faith without wavering; (for He is faithful that promised ;)" – Hebrews 10:23. "Can a woman forget her sucking child, that she should not have compassion on the son of her womb? Yea, they may forget, yet will I not forget". (Isaiah 49:15). Do not quit; God cannot forget you.

Marriage is a covenant; a very serious institution and should be taken seriously. When I met my husband, Femi, he had graduated and worked as a Water and Soil Engineer. I was a secretary, and he loved me for who I was. It is important to ensure that whoever wants to marry you loves you for who you are and that you love whoever you want to marry for who the person is. A happy marriage is work in progress where both parties must be ready to roll up their sleeves to work together. We must commit to working on our marriages. We must be deliberate about it and not take our spouses for granted. Many things will show up; some will be positive, others negative. Our prayer is that the positives will far outweigh the negatives. Above all we need to allow God hold up our marriages for us. Daily praying together is a binding force in marriage. A healthy sex life is a delicious topping in marriage.

With God at the Centre of our union, we daily continue to commit ourselves to God and build our home around His word and His principles. As we let the word of God be the yardstick for the decisions we make in life, our lives have continued to take shape. When conflicts show up, we face them not as competitors but as a team. When things go wrong with either of us, it automatically affects the other. There are no winners and or losers. We are one.

A key aspect in marriage where there should be no winners or losers and two become one is in physical intimacy. Like I said earlier, sex is a delicious topping in marriage. Romance is vital to the success of any marriage. Husband and wife should be naked and not ashamed of their bodies. This part of marriage is largely physical, so there should be no 'over-spirituality' about it. Couples must satisfy each other's physical desires and never take each other for granted. Some regrettably use sex as a weapon of war. This is an ungodly thing to do.

There is also a place for right words in marriage. It is important to be mindful of the things we say to one another. Words and attitudes break more marriages than actions do. Words cannot be retrieved; once spoken, a process begins. God made the world with words. The power of life and death is in the tongue. So, to boost romance, learn to be romantic with words. Give your spouse pet names. Practice celebrating each other, affirming with complimentary words. Do not be frigid; spice up your marriage with words that will cause your spouse to laugh. Allow your home to be filled with excitement.

Our mindset is very important in everything we do so our mindset in marriage is not an exception. Some folks believe that in-laws are generally wicked. My husband and I right from the point of courtship desired a wonderful relationship with our in-laws. For me, it was a tough call. I knew that I would be dealing with more sophisticated, exposed, and highly enlightened in-laws. I was initially scared and concerned about that, especially as my husband was the only male child among four sisters. That meant I would have four sisters-in-law, women of timber and caliber, to relate with.

I felt intimidated by their sterling and solid persona since I was just getting out of a mindset of low-esteem, fear, abuse and timidity. I however anchored my faith on the word of God and strengthened myself in the place of prayers. I made up my mind to win any battle which came my way with the weapon of love. My first two years with my in-laws were quite interesting and I must confess that I learnt, and I am still learning a whole lot from them. An unforgettable drama that readily comes to mind was a day my husband and I alongside his sisters were in his father's house. It was a few months after our wedding and one of my sisters in law in response to a report about what someone did remarked, "that was atrocious!" I looked at her with deep admiration as I secretly scribbled the word "atrocious" on a piece of paper. I did not quite get the correct spelling, but I wrote it out as it sounded and after my husband confirmed the correct spelling, I checked up the meaning. I always loved to hear them speak. I had and still have great respect for them all. I always loved their choice and use of words because they were always additions to my growing vocabulary. Such brilliance and enviable intelligence! My knowledge wasn't as broad, my exposure was limited and there I was, surrounded by more exposed, cultured, intelligent and forward-thinking people. We are all products of influence.

This brings to mind the story of Joseph in the bible. The hand of God was upon Joseph even from childhood. However, Joseph needed that experience as a servant in Pharaoh's household. He needed to go through the travail of life in a prison. That was when he became qualified to become Prime Minister of Egypt. His transformation was so extreme that even his blood brothers could no longer recognize him.

Opening myself up to acknowledging those who knew more than I did, learning from them and cultivating a teachable spirit turned what should have been a burden into a learning process. When I am in the midst of such people, I choose rather to be sincere about my weaknesses and to unashamedly tap from their strength. All of these have contributed to me becoming a better me.

This discovery made me more deliberate in my determination to surround myself with positive, resourceful and inspirational people. Sometimes, such people show up in our lives as unfriendly and difficult bosses, overbearing in-laws, proud colleagues or highly skilled business competitors. Whoever they are, we should see our relationships with them as an opportunity to learn. Remember, nobody has a monopoly of knowledge. Laban in the bible thought he was taking advantage of Jacob, but Jacob refused to be bitter. I learnt a long time ago that if I am bitter, I can never get better.

I am grateful to God that my husband continues to make an amazing job of having my back, covering up my weaknesses and gently yet deliberately challenging me to improve on my best of yesterday. Our marriage is filled with more triumphs than challenges and this is simply because we continue to learn from our mistakes and that of others and never hesitate to ask God for forgiveness whenever we err. Keeping the flame of love alive in a marriage is not automatic. It requires deliberate efforts. It must be worked on by husband and wife and by the grace of God, that flame helps to ward off intruders, strife, boredom, external influence, temptations and the likes. Most importantly, we place a premium on praying together and worshipping God in truth and in spirit.

/////////////////////////////////
Chapter Seven
/////////////////////////////////

My Transition Into Entrepreneuership

fter having both of our children, the decision to go back to work was no longer optional as the buying and selling of everything from clothes to hats to foodstuff to confectionary was not sustainable. Little did I know that taking up a job in Corona School Ikoyi as a secretary was going to be my last bus-stop as far as paid employment was concerned. Life as a secretary in Corona Schools Ikoyi was fun. I enjoyed my job quite well for many reasons, including the fact that our two children eventually became students there. It is very important to have a plan and a picture of what one desires in life. Having a picture has helped my husband and I over the years. This is because life always throws several options our direction and the one thing that enables us to make right choices has been ensuring that we always prayerfully put a plan in place. A plan always serves as a guide. Those plans are however never cast in stone, but they help us navigate and meander our way through difficult times.

Taking up the Corona job when it came was not a struggle even though I had a second option of a job offer at a manufacturing company. The resolve my husband and I made to take care of our children ourselves, pay them maximum attention and shield them from the danger of abuse made the job offer at Corona a wise choice. However, after nine years at Corona, my joy began to dissipate, and I began to feel uncomfortable with where I was. I began to feel there was more to my life than being a secretary at Corona. I fought the feeling because I could not think of an alternative to what I was doing. I felt some sense of security in Corona, but the feeling of discomfort intensified and was almost turning into depression.

I kept praying and hoping this uncomfortable feeling would go away, but it only persisted. I took an inward look at myself – I had no university degree at that time even though I had enrolled and started a part time programme. Unfortunately, at some point after enrolling for the programme, I could not continue because lecture time was conflicting with that of effectively playing my role as a mother. I had no skills I could think of, no capital to start a business. I was totally confused over what step to take. These feelings of dissatisfaction, discomfort and desperation for a change started when I was thirty-eight years old. It appeared my whole life was losing its meaning. I was happily married and our children were doing well but at that point I discovered that what determines fulfilment in life is not in being married or having children but in the discovery of purpose. I began to ask myself the million-dollar question, "what is my purpose in life?" I looked at my life and I felt I had not really achieved much. Though extremely grateful to be alive, though grateful to be very happily married with two beautiful children, I craved for more, I yearned for more, and I hungered for more. "There's oil in your house!", my pastor would preach repeatedly but "I can't see the oil', was my bitter cry.

I refused to give up. I sought counsel, spoke to my husband and finally came up with the plan to resign from Corona to open a Day

Care Centre. I was excited about it initially and began to make enquiries about where I could go for some form of training as I was not ready to put my meagre resources into what I did not have adequate training on. This decision was relatively easy because I had my husband's support. My parents were also very encouraging. I knew they were especially happy to see that I was finally thinking creatively. The blessings from my Pastor gave me a lot of spiritual muscle and I felt very certain that this was the way to go. Regardless of these wonderful people who encouraged me, I had a few well-meaning friends who were quite worried about what my life would become. They knew the real me - my lack of a university degree and my many weaknesses. They felt that a bird in my hand (which was my job) was worth two in the bush and I knew they meant well. However, my wings were already flapping and I was set to fly. I courageously put in my letter of resignation at the end of 2006. As soon as I put in my resignation letter, the reality of the step I had taken dawned on me.

To be able to properly equip myself for my grand plan to set up a Day Care Centre, I enrolled with the Heritage Montessori Centre for a six-month training. The training was intense. The Director of Studies, Pastor Mrs. Adebola Atoyebi was 'energy', personified! You could see passion oozing from her as she facilitated. Her delivery was top-notch and undoubtedly inspiring. I listened to her with hunger. Her experiences were absolutely challenging, and I could also see that this was a woman on a divine mission. I was fired up to fulfil purpose. However, it dawned on me that starting a Day Care Centre was not why God took me to Heritage Montessori Centre. It was simply to sit under the amazing mentorship of Mrs. Atoyebi. At that point, even though I did not quite know what my purpose was, I knew clearly what it was not going into childhood education! God brings people our way or causes us to veer into people's paths for different reasons. Sometimes our perceived reasons for encountering people is not always the intended purpose of God. It is important at all times to be sensitive to God's intended purpose for bringing people into our lives. My emotions were completely mixed, I felt high and dry even though I completed the Montessori program. High because I had become inspired and motivated but dry because I now did not know what next to do. I was careful not to share my confused state with anyone but my dear husband. He was completely understanding and encouraged me to continue waiting on God for direction on my next line of action.

It appeared a long wait. On completion of the training, I knew that going ahead with setting up a Centre was no longer the next step to take. Quietness, serenity, hush was what I needed at that time. I was desperate to know what next. I had tortured myself with numerous thoughts and I knew it was time for me to slam the brakes, take a deep breath and be still. I had to create time to steal away from the crowd, shut the door, draw the curtains and just stay still. I knew I needed to retrospect and introspect before I could prospect. This was a time to forget my achievements, admit my weaknesses and be courageous in the face of failures, challenges and yes, this numbness. I reminded myself of Psalm 127:1 (KJV): "Except the Lord build the house, they labor in vain that build it: except the Lord keep the city, the watchman waked but in vain. It is vain for you to rise up early, to sit up late, to eat the bread of sorrows: for so he giveth his beloved sleep."

I continued to be more mindful of my company. I continued to earnestly seek for people who would add to me, lift me, encourage me, inspire me and most of all challenge me and I found these in a number of my acquaintances.

As we continue our sojourn on earth, having the asset of destiny helpers and destiny collaborators in our lives become essential to us achieving our goals.

Psalms 1:1 (KJV) says: "Blessed is the man that walketh not in the counsel of the ungodly, nor standeth in the way of sinners, nor sitteth in the seat of the scornful."

It was at this point that I decided that while waiting for discovery of purpose, I could in the interim begin to make use of the knowledge gained in my Montessori training.This decision brought two families who wanted their children taken home lessons my way. I gave my all to this service and it did see me through in that waiting period of my life. I realized at that point that waiting does not mean idleness. Waiting means digging deep to use what's available while preparing and looking out for the big break moment.

During this period, I rededicated myself to daily confessing Isaiah Chapter 60 vs 1-22. Confessing Isaiah 60 vs 1-22 was a daily habit I had kept for years but abandoned because I did not see the manifestation of my confession. Little did I know that my divine timing was around the corner. There is no doubt a set time for the word of God to come to pass in our lives.

My set time came but not in a way I expected. It did not come amidst joy, jubilation or celebration. When it came, it found me in pain, full of tears and a whole lot of questions in my heart. I remember waking up that morning and rushing to catch my husband before he left for work to tell him our meal barrel had emptied out and I had run out of cash. I requested that he gave me whatever he had so I could prepare a meal for the family. The calm and loving smile on my husband's face momentarily assured me that I was in for a pleasant surprise that morning. However, my confidence flew out of the window as soon he produced a One Thousand Naira note, held my shoulder and looked into my eyes saying, "go multiply this money, my virtuous wife". I looked at him in utter disbelief and was lost for words. So many negative responses were flying through my mind, but the priceless pre-wedding advice of my late mother turned out to be a firm padlock for my mouth. She had told me before I got married to be careful of what I say in the face of a misunderstanding with my husband. "Take an invisible gulp of water, don't swallow it, hold it in your mouth ... then swallow it when your anger abates", she had told me. I stood transfixed to the spot with tears in my eyes as I watched my husband leave for work. I wondered what I was going to do with the money. All of these were coming at a time we had found ourselves in a state where we didn't know where to start from. Debts had piled up, needs were crying to be met, our entire situation looked bleak and there was that terrible feeling of condemnation because it felt like everyone around us was making progress and we were just stuck in a rut. We however continued to encourage ourselves knowing that the valley situation we had found ourselves was just for a season. We knew we had to be courageous through it all.

Against all odds, I made my way to the market, brainstormed within myself on how best to use the One Thousand Naira and concluded that the only food item I could buy and make into multiple meals was beans. Just as I reached that conclusion, I heard the spirit of God say to me, "make moinmoin today."

After buying some beans, I went ahead to buy other ingredients I needed to make moinmoin and went back home to quickly make the meal before our two children returned from school.

Each time I look back at this stage of my life, I remain grateful for the grace to keep hearing God, for the grace to control my tongue in the face of confusion and the grace to muster courage even in the face of apparent hopelessness. I recall the cry of David in Psalm 46: 3-6: "Though the waters thereof roar and be troubled, though the mountains shake with the swelling thereof. Selah. There is a river, the streams whereof shall make glad the city of God, the holy place of the tabernacles of the most High. God is in the midst of her; she shall not be moved: God shall help her, and that right early."

/////////////////////////////////
Chapter Eight
/////////////////////////////////

What You Release Multiplies

Moinmoin was cooked and you could perceive the aroma even from the stairs. I was glad we would not finish all the wraps I had prepared that evening. That meant I could save another day's meal…or so I thought, until my sister-in-law, Mrs. Olufunto Igun came visiting. It was in vain that I wished she would not question the source of the inviting aroma and I had no choice but to own up that the aroma was from my kitchen. Her request for a taste was reluctantly but surely met. No sooner had she taken the first bite than she asked if I would prepare the same meal for her the next day. Without any hesitation, I obliged, and she gave me a thousand Naira note.

I gladly prepared another set of moinmoin wraps for her the next day. I was left with some wraps after delivering hers. I gave some of my neighbors a few wraps of what I had left while my sister-in-law also shared hers with a friend. Everyone who had a taste of this production just wanted more. That was how I began to receive calls for more and more and more of my moinmoin. This movement is what birthed my company, "NO LEFT OVERS NIGERIA LIMITED".

Life began to have new meaning to me. I would go to bed

exhausted because I was doing what I loved and wake up excited because I was going to do what I loved. It was a simple, ordinary, no frills product but I absolutely loved making it. I loved washing my beans, sorting out my fish, unwrapping my seasonings, washing my pepper and wrapping my moinmoin. Every process was a delight even though it was tedious. The feeling of satisfaction far outweighed the stress and pain. I looked forward to the phone calls, the text messages and the referrals. I began to make money. It was nothing compared to my salary at Corona, but it was mine - my sweat, my labor, my pride - and to crown it all, people loved it. I felt alive, validated and empowered. It was a feeling like none other. Even the love my husband has for me could not compare to that feeling of self-worth. Finally, I felt I had discovered me. I began to brainstorm, I began to read, I began to listen, and I began to desire more. My heart pumped every night, I could not sleep. All I thought about was moinmoin - moinmoin in my prayers, moinmoin in my waking, moinmoin in my rising. Moinmoin became my tagline. Every day I wanted to sell more wraps and tell more people. I had just become consumed by this new life that I had discovered.

The rewards did not come immediately. My husband was super amazing. Olufemi my love! My knight in shining amour, was always supportive of me. When I woke up at 3am to pray before setting out to wash beans at 4am, he would in his sleepy state reach out to me and whisper, "the joy of the Lord is your strength." When it was time to go grind my beans, he would go with me. I cannot forget those early mornings when there was no electricity. My husband would hold a torch, carry my bucket of beans for me and we would walk down to the grinder who was always expecting us. I could never have been able to cope without his support. While I wrapped the beans, he would wake the children and get them ready for school and they all would leave at the same time. These memories just keep me humble and grateful to God for my husband's love, but most importantly for the love of God.

There were tough days – days when we made no sales. I remember the day I had toiled washing beans and just as I finished and was trying to lift my bucket of beans, the bucket handle came off and all the washed beans spilled on the floor. I cried bitterly because I could not imagine starting all over again. My husband came over, looked at the beans on the floor, pulled me into the bedroom, told me to calm down and he went back to pick up the beans. Gains, pains, thrills, frustrations, victories, defeats - these were the roller coaster of emotions I went through even in the triumph of self-discovery. Every day came with different challenges, but I had gotten to the point of no return. There was an untamable rush in me that made me feel I was sitting on something money could not buy. I felt my hair was growing again! I kept telling my husband and children, "I have found my oil; I am pouring out my oil, and I am unstoppable!" I kept pouring and family and friends kept buying. From family and friends, I moved to another familiar environment - my church. I bombarded church members and I could not believe the patronage, my oil just kept pouring and I kept looking for more vessels. Suddenly, it looked like the oil started trickling. It was not gushing out again! Oh God, what is wrong?

////////////////////////////////
Chapter Nine
////////////////////////////////

At The Gate

As scarcity loomed, I began to groan. Fear gripped me. What's happening? What happened to the gush? Is there a blockage, what have I done wrong? Is this testimony going to expire? I asked all these questions in prayers, by examining my product and by following up on existing customers but the orders kept dipping. Some said to me, "my sister has started making moinmoin too." Others would say, "electricity is bad, so I can no longer keep stock in my freezer." All sorts of excuses kept hitting at me and these were having a negative effect on my bottom-line. They appeared like reasons I could not control. I was almost losing my mind; it was like a downward spiral. The fear of going back to the darkness of lack of productivity, confusion and uncertainty gripped me. My husband as usual kept telling me it was a phase that would pass. However, it was a difficult situation for me to accept.

I kept brainstorming and praying on a way forward and I heard a still small voice say, "Go to the gate of Corona School Ikoyi." I was vexed at this suggestion and interpreted it as coming from my desperation, my enemies or the devil himself. However, the more I tried to silence the voice, the louder it got, and I knew clearly at that point that it was the voice of God. I had tried to rationalize within myself how it was going to be a humiliating step to take especially since upon my exit from Corona, I had told everyone I was going to open my playgroup. I dreaded turning up in the school with a cooler of moinmoin and I kept praying that another sales outlet idea would come to mind. It wasn't until I heard that still small voice say, "If you don't go, I will send someone else!" I froze.

I thought it through repeatedly and concluded within myself that I had absolutely nothing to lose. "At least I have something to offer", I muttered to myself, "there is dignity in labor but none in begging."

I spent all night preparing myself for my trip to Corona the next day. My drive down to the school made me feel like a lamb being led to the slaughter. All the 'what ifs' you could think of flooded my heart.

What if I was laughed at? What if nobody patronized me? What marketing tactic would I adopt? What if it rained? "STOP!!!!!!", I had to scream to myself. "Stop and just keep going!" As soon as I did that and kept my mind blank, I had some peace. The scripture in Proverbs 26:13-14 further helped me to keep going: "The slothful man saith, 'there is a lion in the way; a lion is in the streets'. As the door turneth upon his hinges, so doth the slothful upon his bed." I was not going to allow the fear which I knew would paralyze me and get the better part of me.

I arrived Corona School Ikoyi just before school closed so I had enough time to park my car and position myself for visibility. As I stood at the gate, I began to pray that the few friends who had warned me against resigning from my job because I did not have an alternative plan would not show up. The ringing of the school bell signifying the close of school interrupted my thoughts and I stood by as parents, guardians and drivers trooped into different classes to pick up children. A few minutes after, they began to trickle out with the children and I could see one of my friends who had warned me about the dire consequences of leaving the known for the unknown. I suddenly became confused and wanted to walk away before she could catch a glimpse of me. As soon as I took a step back to find a secure hiding place, I looked at my cooler of moinmoin and at that point, the desperation to sell knowing fully well that I had used up all my money to produce the day's moinmoin got the better part of me. Immediately, I reasoned within me and concluded that the best form of defense was attack. I started yelling, "moinmoin for sale, moinmoin for sale, buy this moinmoin and your life will not remain the same again". Everybody around me stopped to take a good look at me and almost at the same time, I could feel someone grab my arm. It was my friend. I could see her concerned look. "Ayo, what are you doing selling moinmoin?" she asked. "What happened to the dream about the school?" I knew there was no time for much talk as I could see parents getting into their cars. I smiled at her and responded, "my friend, the school will come, just buy this moinmoin and experience something new." She dug into her purse and produced money to buy a few wraps, I found myself surrounded by a handful of parents who also wanted to buy. My paranoia disappeared as I became consumed with selling. As I sold, I had to answer quite a few curious parents who asked questions from "are you okay?" or "are you sure about what you are doing?" to "how are you coping with life?" I also got comments from "it is well" and "God will see you through", to "stay strong".

All of that did not really matter to me. All that mattered to me was that I was selling. Wow! Within a few minutes, my cooler was empty, and I had my money in my hands! I could not believe it! Some even came back for more and were extremely disappointed to find out it had finished. I drove back home that day amidst tears of gratitude. I sang my heart out and could not just wait to get home to tell my darling husband and children. They were thrilled! My husband kept saying "that's my girl". After the children went to bed that night, my husband and I sat together and began talking about the different experiences we had had within the almost one year of me leaving paid employment. Quite frankly, it had been like a mad rat race that looked unending.

My daily routine in that season of my life was almost predictable. We recalled that shortly after starting my moinmoin business, to earn a little more income than what was coming in from my daily sales of about five thousand Naira (not profit, but sales), I had taken up two home teaching jobs. My daily routine therefore was to wake up at 4am, have my morning devotion, soak beans in water, get leaves, fish, pepper and other ingredients ready, then wash the soaked beans. My darling husband was always on hand to walk me down the road at 5.30 to grind the beans and as soon as we returned home, I was in the kitchen wrapping moinmoin.

As soon as wrapping was done and the pot covered, I would make a dash for the bathroom, get dressed, and off I went to get an "okada", a commercial motorbike, to take me to the home of two children I had to teach. Thank God for my husband who always ensured he turned off the cooker when the moinmoin was done before leaving for work. My timing had to be perfect to ensure he was not delayed. As soon as I was back from teaching, it was time to begin doing the rounds of delivering moinmoin to my clients. My clients at that time were made up of beer parlor owners, family and friends. That was the crazy daily routine in that season of our lives until schools resumed.

The inspiration to start selling by the gate of Corona School Ikoyi was about to open a new chapter in my life. The reality that no season lasts forever became evident to me. Indeed, seasons come and go. I also became aware of the all-important fact that there is a blessing in every season of life. A lot of times these blessings are disguised. The eyes that see such blessings are those of someone with a positive attitude. Joy filled my heart as I realized that asking God for grace and wisdom to make the best of my present season was the key to divine victory. Indeed, no matter how bad it looks on the surface, asking God to open our eyes to see the honey in our "carcass" situation is the way to go. "I will keep moving", I told myself. The grace and strength I needed in every season came as I moved, and every movement led me into my rest. As I reminisce, I recall again a scripture: "Do you see a man skillful and experienced in his work? He will stand [in honor] before kings; He will not stand before obscure men." -Proverbs 22:29 (AMP).

///////////////////////////////////
Chapter Ten
///////////////////////////////////

Different Stops Before The Palace

O ver the almost three months of standing at the school gate, I had several experiences. I remember ending a phone call by saying "I will rather walk away!". Prior to this phone call, I had been invited by a gentleman who "lured" me into his office under the guise of wanting to buy moinmoin. In his words, "Ayo, I am making you a juicy offer that will change your life. This moinmoin you are selling cannot take you far." I was shocked at the audacity of his statement. He was someone I had great respect for. However, this side of him that was manifesting right before my eyes was different from the revered impression I had of him. Even though I walked out of that meeting making it clear that I was more interested in continuing with my moinmoin business than going into any venture with him, he kept calling to find out if I had changed my mind. I kept picking his calls because in the same breath he would order for more moinmoin and I felt I just needed to be diplomatic, so that I would not lose his patronage.

After days of pestering me despite my efforts to be as respectful as I possibly could, my firm reply of choosing to walk away from the patronage I was enjoying from him became the only option available to me. I knew if care was not taken, I would be distracted. There are times when we must walk away from short term comforts in order to keep our dreams alive. There are times we need to ask God to strengthen us and grant us the courage to walk away from ties and associations that conflict with our dreams in life.

I have also experienced great deliverances from disaster - deliverances that almost made me erroneously conclude that what I was doing was not the way to go. One of such was a day I found myself running frantically to my house. As I ran as fast as my legs could carry me, I did not care what I looked like, who was looking at me or what anyone thought of me. I had forgotten to turn off the gas burner with stew on it. This was a major crisis on my hands and attending to it was my priority at that time. I was still a few meters from home, my legs were weak and my hair disheveled but none of that mattered. Worse still, I had only remembered after about thirty minutes of leaving my house! Even more alarming was the fact that there was heavy vehicular traffic everywhere!

Our children, about eleven and thirteen years old then were in the car with me. On remembering the "burning offering" I left at home, I switched into survival mode, parked my car by the side of the road, prayed over my children, left them in the car and began the about 20 minutes or so "race of life" to my house. I was relieved that I didn't see flames as I approached our building. On opening the door to our flat, the living room was full of thick smoke, the pot was badly burnt and all I could do to avoid the unthinkable was turn off the cooker. God got me there just in time! When I left home, He was with me. While I was driving, He was with me. When I left my children in the car all alone by the roadside, He was with them and while I was running the race of my life to my house, He was there!

Standing at the gate of Corona taught me the importance of punctuality. If I did not get there early I would always miss those parents who picked their children up early. The devastating consequences that could come from lateness became real to me on a boat cruise my husband and I participated in. All participants had been told the departure time way ahead of time, so when the D-day came, my husband and I got there on time especially as it would be the first one we were attending. The boat had its maximum capacity, so limited tickets had to be sold. I remember my husband and I had saved up for our tickets. Everybody wanted to be part of the cruise because a celebrity was going to be on board and he was going to give us all time to interact with him.

The operators had told us that once the boat began to sail, there was no turning back. Those were not the days of mobile phones, so there was no way to call friends who we knew had bought tickets but hadn't boarded. The final call for boarding was made and the boat began to drift off shore. No sooner had we taken off that more people began to arrive. They were waving frantically for the boat to come back, but it was too late. One of the late comers had paid for tickets for quite a number of other people on board but because he was late, he missed the boat.

This incident left an indelible impression on me. May I not, after all my preparations, after all my labor, after all my kindness to others, miss my appointment with destiny. Some were probably delayed because there was traffic, some because they had to get the family ready, others may have been delayed because they didn't have cars of their own to get them to the port and had to hitchhike with people who had no respect for time. Some were perhaps delayed because they had to bring refreshments for others. All had one legitimate reason or the other but faced a common consequence - they missed the boat!

The set of people I was most sympathetic with were those who were late because their carriers had no respect for time. They lamented that they had gotten themselves ready over half an hour before their carriers came. I learnt the valuable lesson never to form any alliance or go into any partnership with people who did not share the same values with me. I will love them but never tie my destiny with theirs. It is always sad to remember the story of the man of God and the old prophet in 1st Kings 13.

All lessons I learnt cannot be written in this book but there is this particularly hilarious one. I remember once refusing to listen to my husband because I felt he was wrong, and I mean, sincerely wrong. How could he see my nicely fitted, beaded sleeveless linen yellow dress as being too tight? This dress was a show stopper. The moment I set my eyes on it, I knew that I just needed to get it. I was a size 10 and the dress was a size 8 but I just needed to get it. "I will slim down into it", I told myself.

After all the hard work of denying myself food and actually losing weight to fit into it, I wasn't going to let anyone stop me. Seeing I wasn't ready to listen, my husband in his usual calm manner said, "OK, you can go." All eyes were on me as I walked to the bus stop. I was convinced they were stares of admiration and exaltation to God for taking extra time to sculpt my body. This dress was just what I needed to "reveal" God's glory.

No sooner had I gotten to the bus stop that a commercial bus going my route stopped. As soon as I got on the bus and tried to make my way to my seat, I suddenly got stuck and I heard the sound of a tear. It was my nicely fitted beaded sleeveless linen yellow dress! The bus had ripped it!

I remembered the scripture in I Samuel 15:22 that says, "Behold, to obey is better than sacrifice, and to hearken than the fat of rams." Amidst rage, fury and sobriety, I made my way back home. Upon telling my husband what happened, he smiled, looked at me and asked, "So what would you like me to iron for you to wear?" Much more than this is the love of Jesus when we go astray. He never discards, He never turns away, He is ever loving and ready to take us back. Have you strayed away from His presence and His will? Do you feel He'll never forgive or love you again? You're wrong. His arms are wide open waiting for you to come home. He's ready to remove our filthy garments and put on us nicely ironed outfits.

I could go on and on with different incidents in my life that have taught me life lessons. I remember once making a frantic call to my neighbor over our street being invaded. I had woken up that morning to hear loud thuds on my roof. Still feeling quite sleepy, I looked through my bedroom window and all I could see were monkeys everywhere!!!! Monkeys were in my compound, on the cars, on my fence, strolling on the edge of my balcony, on the road, in the house across the road, on the poles, on the power cables, monkeys of different shapes and sizes were everywhere! It was such a bizarre and nerve-racking sight.

Over a considerable period, we had observed that two or three monkeys would stray onto our street from the "bush" behind our house. We also discovered that they would sometimes feed on the huge mango tree in our compound, but we paid little or no attention to them until that morning.

This is what happens when we tolerate a little discomfort, a little misfortune, a little disturbance and we do nothing about it, I thought to myself. Immediately, we arranged for our mango tree to be trimmed as we discovered it was a major attraction for the monkeys. I said to myself, "Ayo, let go of trees in your life that attract any form of negativity." Matthew 3:10 (KJV): "And now also the axe is laid unto the root of the trees: therefore, every tree which bringeth not forth good fruit is hewn down and cast into the fire."

Some of our children's experiences have also served as valuable lessons to us, and my husband and I are grateful for the privilege we have been given to raise them in a loving environment. All through our children's years in primary school, my husband would daily lovingly make sandwiches for their break time every morning before they left for school. Even in their 20s today, they fondly remember how they were the envy of their friends because their dad made out time to make their sandwiches daily. "Dad would always cut the bread to precision", they would say. Isn't it simply amazing those little things we do that leave a lasting impression in their hearts? Psalm 37:16: "Better is the little that the righteous has than the abundance of many wicked". Celebrating the little that we have increases the blessings of God in our lives.

I also remember when our son was away in school and I made a phone call to him asking him how he was coping with his school work. He told me of one of the most challenging projects he carried out that semester. He had to construct a model using cardboards and other delicate materials. The project took him weeks of preparation and hard work to complete. He said on completion of the project, he took a step back and felt a huge sense of relief and accomplishment at the outcome of all his hard work. No sooner had he started making his way to school the day after completing his project that a gust of wind swept his project out of his hands! He said he watched in total helplessness as his project went flying across the road. Cars sped past crushing it into pieces!

I had tears in my eyes as he told me how he sat on the pavement with his hands on his head and continued to watch in horror as weeks of hard work littered the streets. Meanwhile, passersby kept going about their normal daily businesses. He ended up repeating the project and completing it in two days. This time he didn't do it from home. He stayed back in school to complete his project to avoid a repeat of what happened with the first one. His project was rated as one of the best in class!

This taught me that no matter how badly life has dealt with me, I can always start again. My heart was full of joy as I ended my call with him. All the pushing and prodding had not been in vain, I thought to myself. Images of how my husband and I used to encourage him flashed through my mind. I remember how we would say to him, "Jump!" and he would respond, "The bar is too high." We kept repeating, "you can jump!". He went ahead, jumped and scaled through. Amazed at his accomplishment, he kept jumping and scaling through. Today, we are grateful to see how well he continues to jump and scale through several other obstacles that confront him. He no longer thinks of retreating especially when he remembers how God has helped him. He continues to summon up courage, confronts obstacles and delightfully overcomes them. We keep watching as he continues to run through troops and leap over walls. We rejoice as we see both our children continue to see themselves as God sees them.

Certainly, one cannot rule out moments of anxiety in raising children. Our daughter once participated in an excursion to

Abeokuta by train and the train broke down in the middle of nowhere. My husband and I stood silently alongside many other parents waiting for the train and as I looked at the time for the umpteenth time, I couldn't believe it was almost I am!

The fact that we could no longer make any phone contact with any of their teachers heightened our fears. "Lord help me", I whispered. My daughter was just 9 years old! At this time, the train terminus was as silent as a graveyard. All the "prayer warrior" parents seemed to have gone on recess. It was such an eerie feeling. Suddenly, the sound of a train tore through the silent night. We all broke into a thunderous applause giving thanks to God amidst tears of joy and relief. We all forgot the pain of waiting. Isaiah 54:4 (KJV): "Fear not; for thou shalt not be ashamed: neither be thou confounded; for thou shalt not be put to shame: for thou shalt forget the shame of thy youth, and shalt not remember the reproach of thy widowhood anymore."

Life lessons are indeed learned daily. I remember taking my daughter out because she wanted a bar of chocolate. We got to the store and I filled the trolley with boxes of chocolates, assorted biscuits, ice cream and many more goodies. She was excited as I gave her the liberty to pick all she wanted. On getting to the cashier, my daughter saw other customers making cash payments. She turned to me and wondered why I was holding a plastic card instead of cash. I tried to assure her not to worry as I had money loaded on my card, but she resorted to throwing tantrums because she did not see anyone on the queue pay with a card. She became afraid that we would not be allowed to leave the store with her goodies and this made me sad because it meant she did not trust me. That day, I realized that this is how we make God feel when He makes promises to us and we refuse to believe Him simply because we don't see things work out according to our expectation.

There are seasons when we are faced with difficult times - the trauma of caring for a terminally ill person, the pain of losing a loved one, the struggle to pay bills, our worries over our health, relationships and the list goes on. There is a tendency to feel all alone. There is that temptation to conclude that we are stuck in a rut. Undeniably, such feelings could be quite overwhelming. However, to keep going at such times, we must remember that as long as there is life in us, there is indeed hope for a brighter tomorrow. 1st Thessalonians 5:24 (KJV): "Faithful is He that calleth you, who also will do it."

I realize that sometimes we try too hard to protect our children. Some of us are so determined to make sure they do not suffer the things we suffered. As wonderful as this sounds, we need to be careful not to play God in their lives. There are experiences we have gone through that have helped in forming character in us and it is important to remember that we cannot shield our children forever. As they grow, we must continue to ask God for wisdom to impact their lives. Now, in their 20s, we know of course that gone are the days of commanding them to sit down! Now, we dialogue. No longer can we stuff things down their throats; they have come of age. My husband and I continue to remind them that life is much more than possessions. Our responsibility when it comes to raising our children is to be deliberate in instilling strong values and God-consciousness in them. There were times our parenting methods were not palatable to our children, but we knew we had a responsibility to continue to do what we were doing and also improve on our efforts. There are times when we would set a whole day aside to wait on God as a family. We needed to let them know that it was possible to survive if we shut out the world for a few hours or even for a whole day and devote time to seeking God's face.

We would go down memory lane of our own growing years with them. The importance of walking away from vanity was one of our emphasis to them. I particularly would tell them of how I felt when I didn't have very nice clothes, and I thought owning them would really be the ultimate. I felt that way concerning a lot of things I didn't have. When I began to have a few nice things, I discovered that owning them never brought complete satisfaction. At man's darkest hour, when the chips are down and life hangs in the balance, the reality of the vanity of life hits you and you conclude that (material) things don't make a man. What makes a man is the spirit of God inside a man. Little wonder why the spirit of depression has no respect for the rich or the poor. What brings about fulfilment in life is the state of the inner man. Is the inner man well fed? Is the inner man healthy? Is the inner man secure?

I have a friend who carries herself with so much poise, elegance and grace. She told me she was schooled to walk with balance in mind. She went through tutorials that included balancing books on her head, looking straight ahead, walking one foot in front of the other, swinging her arms and critically ensuring that the books do not fall, then she learnt to increase her pace till she attained perfection. For proper balance in life's journey, we go through similar tutorials in the hands of our Good Shepherd. He only places weights He knows we can bear on us and tells us to fix our eyes on Him while at the same time ensuring that we continue to gallantly take territories here on earth. I Peter 5:10: "But the God of all grace, who hath called us unto his eternal glory by Christ Jesus, after that ye have suffered a while, make you perfect, stablish, strengthen, settle you."

Regardless of today's struggles, we need to rest, assured that our Good Shepherd will settle us. If we allow what people say about us cage us, we will never know that there is anything called 'greatness' in us. We need to go beyond bothering ourselves over what people say. We need to go beyond condemning ourselves over our past mistakes.

There is so much in us, but we can never see them until we turn our backs on what people say. We can never emerge until we forgive ourselves for past mistakes and embrace the freshness that a new day brings. We need to arise, because there's much more to us than this.

"O thou afflicted, tossed with tempest, and not comforted, behold, I will lay thy stones with fair colors, and lay thy foundations with sapphires." - Isaiah 54:11 (KJV) I am a witness that afflictions fill us with the temptation to abort everything and lash out in anger or cause us to walk away from it all. At such times, I sit back and remind myself of how long it took me to get to where I am right now. When I recall all the pain I had to go through to get here, I realize that I cannot just give up. I look back at those years of praying, waiting, confessing the word of God, enduring and standing against all odds and I have become aware that just one wrong word can mess everything up. I always resort to asking God to grace me with the strength of silence. My prayer has become, "Lord, help me to keep my tongue from evil and my lips from speaking guile." (Psalm 34:13). When the stability we are enjoying in our lives, businesses, career, finances, families and other areas become interrupted and it looks like there is no way out, it is time to stand and see God light our candle and enlighten our darkness. It is like entering a room and finding the room totally messed up. The natural reaction is to feel overwhelmed. Sometimes when you find yourself in such a situation, you might be tempted to call a friend or two to help you out, and there is nothing wrong with doing so. However, there are times when there is no one to call. At some point, everyone appears to be preoccupied with their own issues. What do you do but roll up your sleeves and start the process of tidying up all by yourself. You will be amazed that as you pick up one item after the other, as you clean up space after space, you will begin to see order and then you will appreciate the beauty of your space.

Thinking your life is all messed up? Quit feeling overwhelmed. Ask God for strength to deal with the issues one step at a time and you will be amazed at how His Grace will take over. Push like a woman who is about to give birth after nine months of pregnancy. Push with every strength you have. In due season, that dream will come forth. You will forget all the pain, you will look at that dream and say, "you are worth the pain."

Isaiah 66:8 (KJV): "….for as soon as Zion travailed, she brought forth her children".

I recall my first pregnancy. From the moment I found out I was pregnant, I lived extremely conscious of the fact that inside of me was another precious life. My delivery time came, and I struggled to push. Being a first timer with a 4.2kg baby, an episiotomy was done. Little wonder I struggled to push! I needed extra help for the baby to come forth. The birthing of huge dreams requires helpers of destiny. May our paths and that of our destiny helpers at different seasons of our lives always cross and may they fulfill the purpose for which they come into our lives. Do not give up, that "child" is worth the labor and all shall end in praise.

Different faces, different paths, different story lines I learnt in my confused, dissatisfied and grappling-to-know-what-next state taught me to make multiple variants of lemonade with the lemons life threw my way. This season is no exception and I'll be coming out with another type of lemonade. One thing I vehemently refuse to do is to give up.

Many weeks went by and the chapter of my life at the gate of Corona School Ikoyi was filled with several ups and downs - days of bumper sales, days of selling in tears, days of selling on credit and days of taking moinmoin back home. The few days of taking moinmoin back home were characterized by all sorts of drama on the home front. My children were always traumatized during such periods because they were seasons I would make them eat moinmoin repeatedly to avoid it staying too long in the freezer. "Mummy, please, we don't want to eat moinmoin today!" was their cry on such occasions. I always responded by sternly warning them that it was a sin to refuse to eat what was available. My husband's reaction always brought deep comfort to me even though I knew he also struggled with back to back moinmoin meals during that period. We however remained grateful to God that we were not where we used to be anymore.

I had started reading up on how to succeed in business and how to take my business to the next level. Branding my business became my priority as I learnt that the image I portrayed of my business would determine who patronized me. Weighing my options especially with the meagre resources at my disposal, I decided to quit selling from unbranded nylon bags to selling in branded bags. We had the name of my company 'No Left Overs' and my phone number printed on the bags and little did I realize that this simple move was going to be a catalyst in the hands of God for my next level.

From selling moinmoin at the school gate, people began to ask me if I could prepare other meals like Jollof rice, fried rice, salads and other general meals. I always responded in the affirmative as these meals were everyday meals I could easily make. It wasn't until I started receiving orders for traditional soups from the Eastern part of Nigeria that I started developing cold feet. The first time I got one of these soup orders, I remember asking God what to do. I clearly received instructions to go to the market down the road from my house and there would be someone waiting for me. As soon as I got to the market, I looked straight ahead of me and I walked down that direction. The Holy Spirit led me to a middle-aged woman.

Ordinarily, I would never have been attracted to her. She had a rumpled tee shirt and a faded wrapper on. I was attracted to her because I could see she sold ingredients for soups from the Eastern part of the country. I did not realize my desperation was written all over my face as I stood in front of her stall until she asked for what I wanted. When I told her the soup I wanted to cook, she smiled and told me she observed I was a Yoruba girl and wondered what a young Yoruba girl like me wanted to do with the soup. I kept responding "I have been told to cook it." She laughed and told me she perceived I was married to a man from the Eastern part of the country and my in-laws had probably given me an ultimatum to cook their native soup. My lips were sealed as I watched this woman's drama unfold. She asked if I had writing materials.

Fortunately, I did, and she proceeded to tell me all I needed to buy alongside giving me detailed instructions on how to cook the soup. This woman became my helper of destiny in that season of my life. Henceforth, anytime I had new Eastern soup orders, I would dash to her stall and she was always sure to tell me how to go about cooking them. That was how I learnt to make soups from the eastern part of the country without having to pay a dime or go to a catering school. This experience taught me an unforgettable lesson. We are one, two or three people away from our destiny helpers. They are always near us. I believe what we really need to pray for is the grace to recognize them and the wisdom to relate with them.

My sales drive at the gate continued amidst requests for different meals. One day, as I stood by the gate beckoning on parents to buy moinmoin, I observed a mother who always came to pick her children in the company of security escorts. This day was different however, as the woman walked unaccompanied. Not only did she walk unaccompanied, she had a No Left Overs bag in her hand. My excitement got the better part of me as I welcomed her with a very broad smile and asked where she got the bag she was holding from. It wasn't until I had asked the question that I realized that I was invading her privacy. She obviously was not too pleased by my question but responded by telling me she bought some things down the road and the things she bought were put in the bag for her. Upon her asking me why I wanted to know, I excitedly told her the brand inscribed on the nylon bag was my company. I reeled out all I could cook to her. She listened intently and after I had finished, she asked if I could provide lunch services to one hundred people every day. She said she owned an Oil Servicing Company and they were desperately in need of a caterer to manage their canteen. The caterers they had tried in the past had not been able to satisfactorily meet the needs of staff and they were hunting for good caterers. She said the only snag was that the caterer must be able to prepare soups from the eastern part of the country. I could not believe my ears and excitedly told her I could meet their expectations. She gave me her complimentary card and the following day after seeing the Human Resource

Manager of her company, I was allowed a one-week trial. The one-week trial led to a two-year contract with the company. It was indeed surreal!

All we need for our next level is hidden in our present level. When we maximize the opportunities in our present level, the goldmine that will lead to our next level will show up. Stretch that present level and see your next height show up! With this, I became like Peter who after having toiled all night and caught nothing allowed the master use his boat, and the master ended up giving him much more than he could handle. I began to go around looking for staff to employ to be able to start catering to this organization.

We started off well, but I was still hungry for more. I was hungry for my next level. I was not satisfied. I asked God to give me more. My hunger for more of God and more of manifesting my next level intensified. I knew what would satisfy this hunger was not food or any material wealth. It was a hunger to move from the known to the unknown; it was a beckoning by the Writer of my destiny.

When the hunger pangs initiated by the writer of our destiny to reach out for more in life is mistaken for food and drink, we become prey in the hands of destiny stealers and destiny killers who offer us the "pottage" of life as substitutes for the real thing. When we confuse purpose for the acquisition and accumulation of material wealth then we sabotage our future and end up as slaves. What are those dreams that we have given up on? What are those aspirations we have traded for momentary pleasure? The One who restores wasted years is giving us a unique opportunity to take them back today.

Jesus calls today - answer. Jesus knocks today - open! Jesus reaches out to you today - run into His arms! Fight that fight now, not in the flesh nor with idle words. Remember, 1st Corinthians 4:20: "For the kingdom of God is not in word but in power". Take it back on your knees, hold on to His Word and consistently dwell in His secret place. I knew that this was my major need - to dwell and continue therein. Just the way we love visiting beautiful places and sitting down to take in the beauty that nature brings, God's secret place is a place like none other. It is a place where we experience ultimate joy, indescribable peace, absolute assurance, unending provision, impenetrable security, deep wisdom, unrestricted access and all that we need for life and godly living. To get to that place, we need to get on our knees, yes, on our knees, seek His face, touch His grace and long for more. When we are in that place, we know that all is well. That place is open to you today and the access code is "JESUS".

Part 2

/////////////////////////////////

Chapter Eleven

/////////////////////////////////

From The Gate To The Courtyard

Another chapter of my life and that of No Left Overs started. I became an employer of labor. My staff would resume in our three-bedroom flat every morning. My kitchen was just about 25 square meters. My husband was simply amazing. He accommodated all that I needed to do to get food out of the house to Ikoyi where the office was without complaining. After a few weeks, I had to get one of the cooks to stay with us from Monday to Friday to make the work faster. Our space became invaded. We no longer had the privacy we so treasured. The carpet in the living room was a nightmare. It had permanent foot marks. The kitchen cabinets began to fall apart, the house had a permanent smell of food. Cooking for a minimum of 100 people every day in a residential apartment was no joke but we kept at it. There were days I would be so exhausted and wondered where all these would lead us. Although I had no answers, I kept taking one day at a time. A few months into catering for this company, we got our first wedding contract. It was a huge breakthrough. From this wedding job and savings from moinmoin sales, No Left Overs got her first vehicle. More contracts kept coming and we kept acquiring needed assets to keep the business growing.

As the business kept growing, I discovered more needed to be done. I concluded that starting a business was a lot easier than growing one. When you start with your baby steps and nobody is watching you, your mistakes are not easily noticed, and you can be excused for minor errors. However, as you grow, many eyes start to focus on you. You are no longer easily forgiven. You have to be more deliberate in planning and executing. The business becomes no longer about you. The business now becomes a living entity with a life of its own and needs constant nurturing to continue living. I faced challenges I never saw coming. I realized that the road called success is slippery and if one was not sober and prudent, one could plummet in a twinkle of an eye.

I committed quite a number of blunders that almost snuffed life out of my business. One of such happened soon after the business started doing well when I began to attract all the buy-this-jewelry-now-and-pay-in-five-instalments kind of people. Despite my initial reluctance to buy, this particular jeweler never gave up and like Delilah was in the life of Samson, her continuous marketing wearied me, and I succumbed. It took me about three months to pay for the first set and the compliments I received whenever I wore them emboldened me to take the matter a step further. I bought a few more the next time and of course, this time I got a more expensive set. My jeweler's marketing strategy was to tell me that when all my clients at "CHEVRON and NNPC" saw my expensive jewelry, they would want to patronize me more.

Oh! What a fool I became in that season! I forgot that what brought the clients and patronage was not ultimately in what I wore but in the quality of my service, and in who I had inside of me as a child of God. I defaulted in payment for the jewelry and struggled to pay staff in those months, and guess what? When I went to God in prayers asking for a divine intervention, He told me I had put the cart before the horse. I had to sell off the jewelry to be able to meet my financial obligations at that time. I ended up selling the jewelry at a loss. I had learnt the hard way. I learnt firsthand that to everything there is a season, and a time to every purpose under the heaven (Ecclesiastes 3:1). I learnt a valuable lesson – that gratification must be differed till when it can be conveniently afforded. I have since stuck to living within my means. May God help us to critically and honestly identify when we are the architects of our trials. May He also help us make necessary amends wherever we have gone out of line. A life free from the bondage of impressing others is a liberated life.

After almost a year of my move from the Corona gate to an air-conditioned cafeteria in Ikoyi, I began to have hunger pangs again and I kept praying to God for direction. I began to desire knowledge of how to properly run my business. This desire made me begin a search for an affordable business school. I couldn't believe it when I came across a newspaper advert targeted at women in business who needed training on how to grow their businesses. It was too good to be true. It was just what I needed. I was amazed at how God could be so precise and timely. However, I became intimidated when I found out more about the program. Not only was it a scholarship program funded by Goldman Sachs, a global investment company based in the United States of America, it was a programme that would be facilitated locally by the Enterprise for Development Centre under the umbrella of the Pan Atlantic University. My initial reaction as I showed the advert to my husband was, "Oh Femi! I will not be considered as I do not have a University Degree." My husband responded by encouraging me to forget about what I did not have and concentrate on what I had. I became bold and applied for the program. I was so grateful to God and full of excitement when after two interview stages, I received a letter that I had been selected for the program, and on completion, it would earn me a Certificate in Entrepreneurial Management. My network expanded, my horizon broadened, and my confidence grew.

During this program, I looked forward to case study sessions. It was always interesting to listen to the class analyze, dissect, criticize and appraise other people's businesses. Of course, none of those business owners were there to defend or explain the reasons behind the actions they took. For those whose stories recorded huge successes and continued growth, their deep moments of pain, tears and discouragements were unknown to us. Such moments hardly come to light because they were lonely moments. They were times those entrepreneurs shut out the world and dealt with their challenges. I had continued to experience such moments. I realized that seasons like this will continue to come because they were seasons designed to take me higher. Are you in that season? Don't quit! Psalms 30:5 (KJV) says, "For His anger endureth but a moment; in His favour is life: weeping may endure for a night but joy cometh in the morning."

The program ran for six months and it was absolutely enriching. At the end of six months, representatives of Goldman Sachs came to Nigeria to meet with the first set of beneficiaries of their initiative. We were informed of their coming and a dinner was organized in their honor by the Enterprise for Development Centre. As I settled in my seat alongside other ladies who participated in the program on the evening of the dinner, the Director of the Enterprise for Development Centre Mr. Peter Bamkole beckoned on me and I became rooted to the spot as he whispered, "Ayo, you're going to share your experience with our guests today." My plea to be excused fell on deaf ears. I was very nervous as it would be my first presentation at such an extremely formal and public setting. Thankfully my dear husband was also at the program. When I informed him that I was going to make a presentation, all he said was, "Ayo, just keep connecting with my face." I indeed kept looking at him as I spoke, and his smile and nods of affirmation gave me courage and boldness. I forgot about everyone in the room and passionately shared my experience on the program. The ovation was deafening!

I concluded after that evening that who I focus on would determine how far I go. Isn't it time to take our eyes off our challenges and fix our eyes on our trusted Advocate, Jesus?

Immediately after the program, I got information that the team from the US were interested in coming over to my office the following day. "I don't have an office, I work from my kitchen", I told them, hoping they would change their minds. Surprisingly, my response excited them more and they asked that I expect them by 7.30am the following day. I turned to Mr. Bamkole, "remember I live in Palm Groove and not on the Island?" He laughed and said to me, "Ayo, it's your season - enjoy it." It hit me then that when your season comes, your location can never be a hindrance.

.....AND THE KING'S CHARIOT CAME

Our children were home on holidays, so the entire family was full of joy at the thought of hosting the Americans. My husband became the Director of Affairs that morning as we all woke up early to set up the house as nicely as we possibly could. Still concerned about making sure everyone especially my staff was ready for the visit, my heart almost stopped as I heard what sounded like a commotion from outside. I looked out of the window and was horrified to see armed policemen, cars and commercial buses at a standstill. I also noticed that there were a handful of passersby who were no longer moving. I could hear angry voices requesting to know why traffic was not moving. My conclusion was that the usual commercial drivers' squabble was taking place that morning. "Why have they chosen to cause trouble today when the Americans are visiting?" I asked my husband. Before he could answer, I saw our gates flung open by our security man. He was unusually excited, and I wondered if he had been drinking. Suddenly, I saw three white buses drive in one after the other and there stood my old security man waving his cap in the air and hailing the occupants of the vehicles. As soon as the buses got in the compound, I noticed that the armed policemen proceeded to allow the vehicles that had been at a standstill drive off. Everything unfolded so fast that it took me a few seconds to comprehend what was happening. Oh dear! All of these for me? The armed policemen were the escorts of the Americans! I stood transfixed as I looked out from our flat which was on the third floor. I watched as the buses were being offloaded of cameras and other recording gadgets. "Femi, we have no electricity! How would they power all these gadgets?" This was my frantic question to my husband because we all knew that over the past few weeks we never had electricity in the mornings and the only generating set we had was a 1KVA generator. My husband calmed me down and reminded me that we didn't get them to come to our house by our power. He told me, "let God be God". True to his words, God showed up! As soon as the first American set foot into our flat, electricity was restored! We were stunned beyond words! "God is faithful!", I whispered to my husband!

Pleasantries were exchanged, and they set up their equipment, recording as my staff and I wrapped moinmoin, and interviewing the entire family. In less than two hours, all the drama was over. We were shocked that as soon as they left, electricity went off! Howbeit, we celebrated God's faithfulness and went about our different activities for the day. I could hardly sleep that night. The events of the day kept replaying in my mind. It was a whole lot to take in. I said to myself, "So I really can be sought after?"
I poured out praises and thanks to God for everything - for my life, my family and my new business that was taking such an unexpected leap. As I laid down, I looked at my darling husband who was sound asleep and my mind became overwhelmed with gratitude to God especially for him and for the wisdom God gives at all times.

It was our 15th year in marriage and we had gone through a lot together. I remember times I would be tempted to lash out in anger and God would restrain me. One of such was when we went visiting my parents and my husband parked in a spot I was uncomfortable with. I told him I was uncomfortable with where he parked but he felt otherwise. No sooner had we gotten into the house than we heard a loud bang from outside. We rushed out, and I stood speechless as I looked at the wreckage of the car my husband and our two children had just alighted from. Our car had been hit by a drunk teenager who had taken his mum's car without permission.

A thousand and one thoughts raced through my mind. I was tempted to say, "if only you had listened to me and not parked here this wouldn't have happened!" However, I thought to myself, what good will such a statement make in this circumstance?

Undoubtedly, my husband's heart was filled with remorse already. We returned home that day without a car but with our family intact. A broken and missing car can easily be fixed but the same might not be said for a broken and missing family. We rejoiced, giving praise to God that it did not happen when we were all still in the car. Proverbs 25:11 says: "A word fitly spoken is like apples of gold in pictures of silver." The reverse is, a word wrongly spoken is like apples of silver in pictures of gold. Silver in comparison with gold depicts gloom. Silver apples in pictures of gold will devalue the big picture. I chose the golden apple of silence in the gloomy situation. I chose to be mindful of the golden picture of my marriage above the silver apple that presented itself that day as a wrecked car. God helped me resist the urge to use unfit words that could mess up my marriage.

The pockets of negative occurrences in our relationships are silver apples that need to be injected with fit words. As gold adds value, sparkle and shine to a dull picture so are fitly spoken words in a hopeless situation. Even when we are justified to speak words like "I told you so" in an already hopeless situation, the best thing to do to avert any further crises might just be to play the golden card of silence. After all, The Bible says in Job 13:5: "O that ye would altogether hold your peace! And it should be your wisdom." A fitly spoken word in a hopeless situation turns a hopeless situation into a testimony.

/////////////////////////////////
Chapter Twelve
/////////////////////////////////

Continuing In Growth

L ife and business went on. Diligently and painstakingly, I kept on against all odds. There were good days and there were very bad days but at that stage of my life, there was no going back. I began to see all obstacles as a set up for a promotion. Doors kept opening and shortly after the visit, No Left Overs took the grand step of moving operations out of my home into a rented apartment. It was a major celebration not just for the business but my family. My children heaved a sigh of relief. "Now we have our lives back", they said.

A few months later, I received a mail from Goldman Sachs inviting me to the US to share my story with their stakeholders. That was the beginning of another season in my life. It was an unforgettable trip. My children's faith became strengthened. My husband stood solidly by me and kept telling me, "Ayo, this is just the beginning." On getting to the US, I went through short trainings on how to make speeches and presentations. I had to be schooled because I would be speaking to their executives in the US and in other parts of the world. It looked like a dream. I remember calling one of my friends on arriving the US and she just could not get over the story of my life. I remember she was one of those who used to tease me way back about my skin. I used to be taunted as a young girl. They nicknamed me "leopard skin". My skin was and is still very sensitive. I used to suffer intense torture from sandflies. It was a nightmare. They would feast on my legs with reckless abandon and I would scratch till my legs got swollen. Sadly, all that resulted in blisters of different sizes. As I listened to my friend express shock and gratitude to God for my life, I smiled at myself as I looked down at my legs. These same "leopard-skinned" legs had started taking giant strides and taking me from glory to glory regardless of everyday circumstances that tried to harass me. Somebody reading this needs to receive strength today. Psalm 66:12 (KJV) says: "Thou hast caused men to ride over our heads; we went through fire and through water: but thou broughtest us out into a wealthy place." God delights in turning our mess into a series of inspiring messages. Don't cower under. Eye-popping and mouth-gaping testimonies will emerge from what appears messy today.

A few months after my return to Nigeria from my first trip to the US, I received another letter. This time it was from the Clinton Global Initiative. The initiative was focusing attention on Women Empowerment and wanted to showcase a success story from the Goldman Sachs 10,000 Women Initiative. I arrived the US a few days before the program. On the day of the program, I woke up and felt a bit nervous but committed everything to God in prayers. I could see my chauffeur waiting as I approached the hotel lobby. I slipped into the car, lifted my chin up and was confident that if God could bypass all the filth of my past and overlook my weaknesses, then it was going to be a great night.

As I sat in the hall with world leaders, I kept saying to myself, "this can only be God!" When it was time to make my presentation, I was introduced by Nobel Peace Prize Recipient, Muhammed

Yunus, a Bangladeshi social entrepreneur, banker, economist and civil society leader. Talk about kings being your nursing fathers! I ended my speech and I couldn't believe the standing ovation was for me. I was overwhelmed by all the hugs and kind words from people I never imagined I would meet in my lifetime. As guests queued to congratulate me, an elderly white American woman walked up to me. Her voice was barely audible. She pulled me to herself and whispered into my ear, "God said to tell you He is going to use you." My heart almost stopped beating! I looked at the elderly woman. I was shaking all over. She hugged me, gave me a warm smile and disappeared into the crowd. I will never forget that encounter.

I was living my dream! Friends, God has an end-time agenda. In that agenda is a critical mass of people from different tribes, tongues and nations. He will pass them through the waters, but He will be with them. He will pass through the rivers, but the rivers shall not overflow them. They will walk through the fire and the fire will not be burned, neither shall the flame kindle upon them. These are people whose testimonies shall astonish the world and draw millions to Christ - people who are not ashamed of the gospel of our Lord Jesus Christ. I am a very vital part of that critical mass. Be encouraged my friend; you will come out like pure gold. That pain of today will be the rod in your hands tomorrow to show to the world that Jesus is Lord.

It is indeed time to lay aside the shame of the past. As a young girl, my place of solace after all the bullying, oppression, and pain was in front of my mirror. I would stand in front of my mirror and make speeches upon speeches to an imaginary audience. I was stunned as the memories flashed through my mind. God indeed prepares us for the palace.

79

I came back to Nigeria and kept building the business. There were times when family needs clashed with business and I knew that I had to get my priorities right. Family always came first. I knew that if anything happened to my family, I would not be able to stand. That is my bedrock and I was mindful to put my husband first. This was however easy because I am married to a very supportive and secure man. I remember times we would both get invited to speak at programs and he would be asked how he copes with his wife's popularity. He simply answers, "we are collaborators and not competitors; her success is mine and mine is hers." What a man! At this point, I would like to encourage couples. You are one and there is no need for rivalry or competition in a marriage. There is no need for one partner to feel inferior to the other. We need to see ourselves as blessings to one another. The moment we begin to see ourselves as being in competition with one another, we open the door for the intruder. We need to both be responsible and lay aside all selfishness. Never take advantage of each other's weakness. Would you like to know the truth? My husband and I both have our weaknesses, but we cover each other up. I know his and he knows mine too (and are they many!), but we help each other. There have been a few times when we did not know how to handle issues and we had to seek for help. We sought for counsel from TRUSTED people. We prayed about them before we went to them and God has been our help. We have stumbled a few times, but we get up together. We forgive each other while making a conscious effort not to hurt each other again. We pray together, we share communion every morning and we have great respect for each other. If God can do it for us, He can much more do it for you only if you both let Him. Marriage is a covenant and it takes covenant habits to preserve it.

Chapter Thirteen

And The Beat Goes On

Ontinue, continue, continue! That is the secret to continued success and growth. For as long as there is life in us, there are higher levels to attain. Even when we are old and grey, there is a higher level. My mother died at the age of seventy-five but before she died, she was consistent, even though there was no business she was running or a career she was pursuing. She continued seeking the Lord, she continued praying, and she continued exercising her faith over her husband, her children, her grandchildren and everything under her covering. My father is eighty-two and I remember how my daughter frantically called me when she saw my dad following her on Instagram! "Mum! What's grandpa doing on Instagram?" Never stop continuing until the Lord calls you home.

The invitations to share my story keeps pouring in from different organizations and all the time, I learn deep lessons. Another unforgettable experience was when I received an invitation to be a panelist at the 2nd Global Entrepreneurship Summit in Turkey. I was extremely excited and did not take a second look at my ticket when it was sent to me. Just as my husband was taking me to the airport, he asked to take a look at my ticket. "Wow! You're flying Business Class to Turkey!" I was elated. I recalled that before then, each time I boarded a plane, I would stylishly touch the business class seats and confess that someday, the Lord would upgrade me. The stress of getting to the airport that day made me forget I was holding a Business Class ticket. Overwhelmed by the rowdiness at the airport, I became anxious and panicky. While on the long queue, I saw a couple being ushered to check in at a relatively empty counter. That got me infuriated. I walked up to the airline staff who attended to them and I demanded to know why they were given preferential treatment. "Madam, I'm sorry, they're flying Business Class!" That was when it hit me like a ray of sunlight that I had a Business Class Ticket! When I showed the young man my ticket, he exclaimed, "but why were you on the queue?!"

Too often, life deals with us so unfairly that we forget our identity. Circumstances hit us so severely that we stay numb even when our lives have been upgraded. We get so consumed by the happenings around us, get angry and jealous of those living a better life and we completely forget who we really are. Who are we? The answer is in I Peter 2:9: "But we are a chosen generation, a royal priesthood, a holy nation, a peculiar people; that we should shew forth the praises of him who hath called us out of darkness into his marvelous light." This is an unchangeable identity, handed over to us by THE unchangeable God. Regardless of what circumstances are saying, it's time to leverage on our true identity.

No Left Overs keeps growing to the glory of God and our standard of living keeps improving. I remember when my husband and I began to travel together. We kept looking forward to travelling with the children and it came to pass. It was like a dream! I kept pinching myself and checking our tickets and passports almost daily. I couldn't help fighting my tears as our plane took off.

My deep thoughts were interrupted when my husband squeezed my hand. I looked at his ever calm and smiling face. Trust him to always stay calm, never dramatic. I am always the drama queen of the house.

There is a flight we all should much more look forward to. This flight is not controlled by man. It will be piloted by the maker of all things Himself. That one flight can never be hijacked by terrorists; that one flight can never crash; that one flight will fly beyond the skies! It will fly us to a city whose builder and maker is God Himself, paved with gold and filled with mansions. I look forward to that city; I look forward to that trip, and I jealously guard my ticket, visa and passport which are all embodied in my faith in Jesus. Come what may, I will not drop my faith, I will yet trust Him. Though the global business climate be tough and my body groans under the weight of all the cares and roller coaster of events around me, my faith in Him will not waiver. Men may hate you without a cause, that dream spouse may be delayed, the child may tarry in coming, you may feel pain in your body, you may experience tough financial situations, a turbulent marriage, and more, but God will come through. Let us take this walk of faith together. Let us hold the confidence and the rejoicing of our hope firm unto the end and as we look forward to this most important flight. My prayer is that we will not miss it in Jesus name.

My life's journey is full of testimonies of God's goodness. When I started my entrepreneurship journey, what I was looking for was money, but I found much more! I got what money could not buy - I met with honor. Honor causes Gentiles to come to your light and kings to the brightness of your rising. I have learnt that the man to whom God bequeaths honor shall most definitely be full of riches.

Proverbs 8:18 says: "Riches and honor are with me; yea, durable riches and righteousness." My prayer always is, "Lord, let your Honor never depart from me."

Doors keep opening and I know that they are for assignments God wants me to take up. I am nervous sometimes when I walk up some stages. I remember being in class way back in my primary (elementary) school. Our class teacher had just stepped out and we were all making a lot of noise. Suddenly our teacher walked back into the class looking as furious as a fire-breathing dragon. "All you know to do is to make noise. I have your composition scripts in my hands and you all performed below expectation - yes, all of you except Ayo." Before making this statement, he had ordered us all to stand with our arms raised above our heads. As soon as he concluded his statement, he asked me to sit down and the others to remain standing. Unbelievably, I refused to sit down. The reason was because right behind me in class that day were two girls who were bullies. I knew that if I dared sit, they would deal with me after class. My teacher was perplexed that despite repeating himself severally, I still stood with my hands raised like a zombie.

Those two girls bullied me all through my years in primary school and my academic performance was severely affected. I dreamt of becoming an orator. I dreamt of giving speeches, so from a young age, I paid attention to English as a subject. I remember standing for hours in front of mirrors giving imaginary speeches and engaging in imaginary discussions. However, it appeared as though that dream was never going to come to pass!.

Decades after, the bullies have gone their ways and to the glory of

God, in God's time, by God's design I continue to find myself on platforms I do not qualify for.

In 2014, I became burdened on the need to expand my business further. I prayed hard about it and approached my bank for a facility to open a new branch of my business. My bank however declined to give me the facility I needed. Instead, they offered to give me 30% of the amount I requested for if I had 70%. I was extremely disappointed. About two weeks after this incident, I received a call from Goldman Sachs. They requested to know if I had been able to access any funding to grow my business. When I told them my ordeal with my bank, they responded by telling me that the White House in celebration of International Women's Day was focusing attention on the need for women to be able to easily access capital to grow their businesses. They said the needed to have two women share their stories - one that had been successful in accessing capital and another that the banks had shut the door in her face. This "turndown" by my bank was what qualified me to be invited to speak at the White House on International Women's Day, to share my story and emphasize the need for women to be able to easily access capital to grow their businesses! I have become extremely passionate about women empowerment, poverty alleviation and promotion of gender equality.

What do I say about the rare privilege I had in 2016 to speak alongside Mr. Warren Buffet at the United State of Women Conference in Washington? I also had the great honor of welcoming to the podium the First Lady of the United States of America, Mrs. Michelle Obama at the dinner that rounded off the conference. Not only did that happen, No Left Overs moinmoin was on the menu that evening and yes, Michelle Obama tasted it!

Who says dreams don't come true? They lied! He did it for Joseph and many more, He is doing it for me, and He will do it for anyone who believes in him. That uncomfortable situation is just a phase and you will come out of it. Let no one kill that dream. Once you identify the dream killers, stay away from them. Remember, you will never reach your destination if you stop and throw stones at every dog that barks (Winston Churchill). Never give up on your dream, "for with God nothing shall be impossible" (Luke 1:37), and when God does it for you, never ever hide your story and your testimony. Think of the flip side - the shame, pain, embarrassment or humiliation you would have faced if Christ had not come through for you. If Jesus can trust you to blow the trumpet of His goodness to you in Zion and the alarm of His faithfulness to you on the mountains, He will keep doing more.

I was waiting in the VIP lounge of the Domestic Wing of Muritala Muhammed Airport to board a flight to minister in Enugu when a young man approached me to patronize him (he sold music gadgets). I listened intently as he pitched his business and as soon as he was done, I also pitched the testimony of God's goodness in my life to him. He laughed in such a manner that delighted my heart and made me more determined to tell him about my Jesus.

Still wondering whether to believe me or not, I told him to bring out his phone and search for "the moinmoin woman". By the time the search results came out, you should have seen the shock, reverence and excitement on his face.
He in turn gave me a summary of his life's sojourn and testified that his encounter with me had further deepened his resolve to serve God with all His might. I didn't only buy his product, I gave him

what money can never buy. Never underestimate or belittle anything that God has done for you. It is in spreading the Good News of Jesus that He blesses us more. Revelation 12:11 (KJV): "And they overcame him by the blood of the Lamb, and by the word of their testimony; and they loved not their lives unto the death."

When I was much younger, I used to be really bothered about what people thought about me. I was very timid and insecure. I had no identity or self-confidence. But now, I can boldly say, "thanks be to God who always causes us to triumph in Christ Jesus!" (2 Corinthians 2:14). I know who I am, so what people say cannot matter to me anymore. We need to get to the point where we refuse to allow failures of yesterday define us. Life can only be lived to its fullest when we are rooted in God and trust Him, and when we believe in ourselves and refuse to allow anyone define us otherwise. It is in doing so that we will break boundaries and overcome limitations. Let no man determine your future. Take charge of your life!

Nevertheless, we will always get to some seasons of our lives where we remember that we all have a certain form of 'nakedness'. By nakedness, I mean that everybody has a weakness. Everybody has a limp. Sometimes, we look at successful people and erroneously believe that they have it all put together. The truth is that no one does. God brings people into our lives at different times to help us cover our nakedness, someone we can lean on so our limp is not visible to all. However, we sometimes become too conscious of our limp and we become afraid to reach out for fear of embarrassment or exposure. I know how it feels to be betrayed; I have been there before. I have had in my past, hurtful moments of showing my 'limp' to someone only to have them go to town and shout out to everyone, "hey! haven't you noticed Ayo's limp?" I am a wiser person today. I do not open up to just anyone. I consciously and constantly pray that God will yoke me with trusted men and women and rid me of strange children whose mouths speak vanity and whose right hands are hands of falsehood.   We need people, albeit the right people. We should not let the bad experiences of yesterday turn us into hermits and make us miss out on the people God has ordained to help us get to our next level. We need to pray about our relationships. We need to pray for sensitivity and discernment on who should, and who should not be in the present chapter of our lives.

It's time to silence those voices of fear, doubt and unbelief and enter the great doors that are before us.
Revelation 3:8 (KJV) says: "...... I have set before thee an open door, and no man can shut it"

As we continue to experience God in different areas of our lives, one of our greatest triumphs is watching our children grow in God. We continue to carry our children along in our walk with God and as a result, they get to also experience God by themselves. I believe this should be the prayer of every parent – that our children should know God by themselves, encountering challenges and seeing God come through for them. We have been graced to model Christ to them and they are daily experiencing Christ by themselves. We are therefore delighted that they are beginning to have their own stories to tell. I recall a particular year my husband and I were on vacation outside Nigeria and it felt so good not to have to wake up early in the morning to rush off to work. The more I tossed and turned, the more convinced I felt to stay in bed. I looked at the time and it was 5am. I rolled over not feeling the need to pray as early as I usually did. On second thought, I jumped out of bed knowing fully well that the devil never goes on vacation. The Bible says in I Peter 5:8 (KJV): "Be sober, be vigilant; because your adversary the devil, as a roaring lion, walketh about, seeking whom he may devour."

I struggled with sleep as I started praying. Shortly after praising, worshipping and just basking in God's presence, I had a burden to pray earnestly for our son's academics. I shared this burden with my husband and we both prayed about it. Our son was in his second year in a University in Nigeria then. We were mindful that he needed our prayers and emotional support, because he was repeating a year in school at the time.

About three months after our vacation, the unexpected and undesirable happened. As a result of our son's non-improvement in his academics, he was told to withdraw from school. Three years had been spent in an expensive university and it appeared as though there was nothing to show for it. Our son was distraught, deflated and on the verge of depression. The fact that God had earlier given us a burden to pray for him in this direction helped to prepare us for this development. My husband and I stood by him like a rock encouraging him that the situation at hand was not the summary of his life, but just an incident preparing him for his promotion.

God gave great grace and direction on what to do. God's instruction to send him out of the country was not financially convenient but we took the first step and help kept coming.
To the glory of God, on resuming his new college his grades were

constantly high and his name came up on the Dean's list at the end of each semester. Today, he has graduated with honors from his first program and we return all the glory, adoration and thanksgiving to God.

This experience has strengthened our son's faith in God. He knows that if God does not save from trouble, just like the three Hebrew boys in The Bible understood, He will save in trouble. He is God and He always knows what He is doing. He will take glory in that situation. We rejoiced when we heard our son say, "Mum, dad, the stone which the builders rejected has become the Chief Cornerstone." This taught us an unforgettable lesson. The best time to prepare for war is in the time of peace. We thank God for beautiful and peaceful marriages, successful businesses and careers, well brought up children and the many victories around us. However, we need to take heed at all times. The season of peace and calm is the most appropriate time to be on the offensive against downward trends and unforeseen "kill joy" occurrences.

This must have been the mindset of Job. After seasons of feasting by his children, The Bible records in Job 1:5 that "Job sent and sanctified them, and rose early in the morning, and offered burnt offerings according to the number of them all." Little wonder Job could stand in the days of his affliction and say, "Though He slay me, yet will I trust in Him" (Job 13:15). The Bible says in Matthew 13:25, "But while men slept, his enemy came and sowed tares among the wheat, and went his way." May we never be at ease in Zion.

Our daughter has had her own experiences too, one of which stands out beautifully. She had desired a graduation gift since she graduated from the University. Her desire was an all-expense paid trip to Dubai. My husband and I kept encouraging her to pray about it as it was not part of our immediate plans. I don't think there was any day that passed without our daughter hounding us on this desire. She so tormented us with her desire to the point that I started having dreams of both of us in Dubai!

So, on this particular Sunday morning, she kept singing the anthem, "I want to go to Dubai." Just as she got to church, the Pastor said God was telling him that there was someone in the service who had been dreaming of going to Dubai. Specifically, he said the person still spoke about going to Dubai that very morning, and he requested that that person stand up. My daughter was the only one in the entire congregation that stood up! That was how God visited her with a free ticket to Dubai!

Talk about the power of desire and defiance! Our faith was further strengthened to continue to trust God even in times when nothing appeared to be happening. 2 Kings 3:17 (KJV): "For thus saith the Lord, Ye shall not see wind, neither shall ye see rain; yet that valley shall be filled with water, that ye may drink, both ye, and your cattle, and your beasts."

I also had no choice but to work on my parenting style. I had to quickly transit from my "helicopter mum" style to what I call the "long-leash parenting" style. "They are young adults now", my husband would say each time I tried to poke my nose into their businesses. With both of them almost always physically far from us, still loving the Lord and holding on to the godly values we raised them with, we can truly testify that "Except the LORD builds the house, they labor in vain that build it: except the LORD keep the city, the watchman waketh but in vain." (Psalm 127:1 KJV). Our seeds shall be mighty upon the earth in Jesus' name.

////////////////////////////////
Chapter Fourteen
////////////////////////////////

My Creed

What keeps me going? I have an assignment. Who sent me? My creator, my God. Who equips me? The one who sent me. Will I get tired? Yes, because I am human. Will I be afraid? Yes, that's why He warned me severally in The Bible, the operations manual of my life, "fear not". Will there be obstacles? Yes, but they are stepping stones to my next level. Will I give up? No; I've come too far. What next? I go forward! Will I fail? Not on the watch of my Jesus! I fear not! When the Bible says in Romans 8:28 (KJV), "And we know that all things work together for good to them that love God, to them who are the called according to his purpose", we ought to believe it. God says what He means, and He means what He says. Keep the faith because head or tail, we win in Jesus name. Do not despair; the pain of today will turn around into great testimonies. Many out there will hear yours and will receive strength and encouragement to push through the challenges and obstacles of life. Dear child of God, I challenge you to keep seeking for that which only God can give, and He will cause even Kings to be your nursing fathers.

Psalms 121: 1-2 (KJV): "I will lift up mine eyes unto the hills, from whence cometh my help. My help cometh from the Lord, which made heaven and earth." Our sojourn to the destination called

"Fulfillment of Purpose" is one that requires great faith. Many times, we get discouraged when our finances are low, when there seems to be no support, when complaints from customers are on the increase - the list goes on.

Discouragement happens to everybody. Life happens to everybody. What do you do at such times? Take your eyes off the discouragement and focus on your journey. Encourage yourself in the Lord, learn needed lessons and keep moving.

I pray that the grace that makes following, obeying and understanding God's direction and path for our lives easy will rest on us. Ist Peter 5:10: "But the God of all grace, who hath called us unto his eternal glory by Christ Jesus, after that ye have suffered a while, make you perfect, stablish, strengthen, settle you".

The End

Summary
———෬ළ෬———

Ten years ago, I started the year in confusion, despair, discouragement and total discontentment with where I was. I was sad that at 39, I wasn't sure of what I was meant to be doing. I didn't believe in myself let alone getting others to believe in me. I prayed hard and cried a whole lot. All I could feel was this huge void - a hollowness that was yearning to be filled.

I was, and I still am very happily married; had and still have two amazing children that brought and still bring so much joy to my heart. I had nice shelter, we could eat three square meals, I was and still am a covenant child of God but there was a deep feeling that there was more to my life than all these.

It became clear that as much as marriage is beautiful, marriage does not translate to fulfillment in life. As much as having children is such an amazing blessing, bearing children does not birth destiny. As much as being able to afford the basic necessities of life gives a measure of security, it does not translate to rest.

I asked God for the way out and He promised me He would lead me if only I would trust ALL His instructions. I committed myself to trusting Him while at the same time telling Him how frail I was since I was a mere mortal.

He started me off with an unlikely One Thousand Naira seed which I used in making moinmoin. This unlikely seed birthed a catering company called NO LEFT OVERS and the miracle birth of NO LEFT OVERS caught global attention. I have over the past 10 years of nurturing my "miracle baby" beckoned on partners like Peter in the Bible did.

My journey continues and my partners and I forge ahead to ensure continued growth, sustainability and innovation.

Today, "I look up to the hills; from whence comes my help?" As I leave the day to day running of NO LEFT OVERS into the hands of "Divine Partners" for other assignments, I am confident that my help comes from God.

I speak to the lion in the heart of somebody out there today. Your life was paid for by the blood of Jesus. Do not allow challenges, setbacks, mistakes of the past or anything for that matter whisper to you that you are less than you are! I urge you today to lay aside relationships, habits, attitudes, thoughts and anything and everything that is speaking contrary to your true position as a new creature in Christ Jesus, so you can indeed birth the purpose for which you have been created. Romans 8:14: "For as many as are led by the Spirit of God, they are the sons of God."

Printed in Great Britain
by Amazon

61469974R00061